Praise for *Social Business by Design*

"*Social Business by Design* easily earns a 'like,' a tweet, a follow, a share, a 5-star rating, and plenty of fans. It shows leaders how to transform their businesses and brands using internal and external social media at scale. What could be more urgent or timely?"

—**Pete Blackshaw**, global head, digital marketing and social media, Nestle; author, *Satisfied Customers Tell Three Friends, Angry Customers Tell 3,000*

"Business is changing right before our very eyes. We are in a world of empowered individuals with reliable, always-on, cross-media connectivity with a vivacious appetite for continuous improvement to win amongst global competition. The frameworks in this book dimensionalize the socially enabled cross-functional business-critical opportunities and will help you quickly chart a clear course for success to win in our evolving social business landscape."

—**Michael Donnelly**, group director, worldwide interactive marketing, Coca-Cola

"Every business must find its way forward in today's rapidly changing world. This book details the very notion of what being social means in a new way that avoids the hype. Instead, a fascinating case is made for transforming what organizations can do with social media."

—**Kirk Kness**, vice president of emerging solutions group, T. Rowe Price

"The business world as we know it is changing, and Peter Kim and Dion Hinchcliffe, along with the rest of the Dachis team, are leading the way! The key is understanding how the world is changing and how your business can lead the way. *Social Business by Design* will help guide you."

—**Frank Eliason**, senior vice president of social media
at Citi; author, *At Your Service*

"Launching new social practices in a big organization like L'Oréal requires a strong mind change in which Peter has been our coach: *Social Business by Design* sets the stage of a global marketing change, which is above all, a change of marketing mindset"

—**Georges-Edouard Dias**, senior vice president,
digital business, strategic marketing division,
L'Oréal SA

"*Social Business by Design* gets right to the heart of the social business trend. Dion Hinchcliffe and Peter Kim reveal not just what you need to do, inside and outside your company, to make social technologies pay off—they also show how to put it all together into a cohesive framework and measure the results. A must-read."

—**Josh Bernoff**, senior vice president, idea development,
Forrester Research; coauthor, *Groundswell* and
Empowered

Foreword by Jeff Dachis
Founder & CEO, Dachis Group

SOCIAL BUSINESS BY DESIGN

transformative **social media strategies** for the connected company

DION HINCHCLIFFE
PETER KIM

JOSSEY-BASS
A Wiley Imprint
www.josseybass.com

Published by Jossey-Bass
A Wiley Imprint
One Montgomery Street, Suite 1200
San Francisco, CA 94104-4594—www.josseybass.com

Jossey-Bass books and products are available through most bookstores. To contact Jossey-Bass directly call our Customer Care Department within the U.S. at 800-956-7739, outside the U.S. at 317-572-3986, or fax 317-572-4002.

Wiley also publishes its books in a variety of electronic formats and by print-on-demand. Some material included with standard print versions of this book may not be included in e-books or in print-on-demand. If the version of this book that you purchased references media such as CD or DVD that was not included in your purchase, you may download this material at http://booksupport.wiley.com. For more information about Wiley products, visit www.wiley.com.

Library of Congress Cataloging-in-Publication Data
Hinchcliffe, Dion.
  Social business by design : transformative social media strategies for the connected company / By Dion Hinchcliffe and Peter Kim ; Foreword by Jeff Dachis.—First edition.
    pages cm
  Includes bibliographical references and index.
  ISBN 978-1-118-27321-0 (hardback); ISBN 978-1-118-28362-2 (ebk); ISBN 978-1-118-28510-7 (ebk); 978-1-118-28613-5 (ebk)
  1. Social media—Marketing. 2. Strategic planning. I. Kim, Peter, 1974- II. Title.
  HF5414.H56 2012
  658.8'72—dc23

2011052639

Printed in the United States of America
FIRST EDITION
HB Printing   10 9 8 7 6 5 4 3 2 1

CONTENTS

FOREWORD

Everything that can be social will be.

I firmly believe that's the mantra of twenty-first-century business and the key concept that we must all internalize to achieve our best possible futures. Operating our businesses through a social lens presents a profound new way of thinking. Some of you will know that this trend is something now called *social business*. Most companies are taking steps toward social business, some slowly and some more rapidly. Yet virtually all organizations today need a way to make the changes on their own terms, in a way that gives them a safe path forward that ensures success. *Social Business by Design* offers you that guided route forward, step by step.

When I cofounded Razorfish as the first major digital agency back in the 1990s, it quickly became clear to me that dramatic change was difficult for large companies; it's never easy making the first move toward a fundamentally new, better way of working, thinking, and living. Fortunately, the case for *why* and *how* to effectively adopt social business is definitively and compellingly explored in these pages by my industry colleagues, as well as friends and coworkers, Dion Hinchcliffe and Peter Kim. I've seen both of them grapple with the enormity of the task that lies ahead of virtually all organizations today: to connect business clients with the whole of the developed world using social media, engage deeply with customers and partners in potent new—yet unfamiliar—ways, and innovate and cocreate a more effective way of working that's not just novel but more satisfying, richer, and, yes, profitable for all concerned.

Uncertain economic times can have a chilling effect on innovation and the readiness for the bold moves required to lead an industry in this century. Many companies also have a hard time making the leap to new digital business models. For every SAP, IBM, or Amazon, a hundred companies are struggling in the shadows. But the writing is on the wall. I can read it clearly as a CEO, as can most of my peers in organizations large and small around the world: as you read this, the way we run our organizations is in the midst of changing dramatically.

The implications for social business transformation are writ large. Customer engagement is moving from relatively isolated market transactions to deeply connected and sustained social relationships. This basic change in how we do business will make an impact on just about everything we do. It affects where sustainable creativity and ingenuity are sourced. It defines how productive and rewarding results are created in the form of break-out new products, services, and operational constructs. And for the CxO in all of us, it also means that we now possess major new ways of driving growth, revenue, and margin. Distributed technologies operating in an open ecosystem and placed in the hands of constituents can be leveraged to create and capitalize on emergent outcomes.

It's clear to me that social media have moved far beyond a means of staying in touch with old friends and colleagues. They have become how business gets done. They have also created a highly competitive weapon in the arsenal of those who want to achieve dramatically better marketing, sales, customer service, product development, and worker productivity. The comprehensive vision that Dion and Pete lay out in this book explains exactly why organizations need to commit to the path of social business in order to survive and thrive in the very different conditions of this new millennium.

In these pages, you'll see how successful companies go outside their comfort zones to embrace new consumer methods of social media and social networking, enabling them to accomplish business objectives in revolutionary new ways that are much more scalable, efficient, and robust than in the past. Some of these featured companies are the most respected names in their industry, and others are disrupting industries and starting their own rise. Yet these stories will also be your stories, and it's how you'll get there too: by a process of deliberate, intentional transformation.

For our part, Dachis Group believes strongly in the full-strength vision of social business as the way that organizations will work now and in the future. I invite you, after reading *Social Business by Design*, to continue your explorations of this topic in our Social Business Council and track your organization's progress as it makes the transformation to the twenty-first century using our Social Business Index, our strategic online service that helps companies measure how effective their business is at being social. It can be found at http://socialbusinessindex.com. These are very exciting times indeed, for organizations that are prepared to build the road ahead.

Austin, Texas   Jeff Dachis
February 2012

SOCIAL BUSINESS BY DESIGN

INTRODUCTION

Ask just about anyone today about social media, and they will probably acknowledge using Facebook, knowing something about Twitter, and admit that social media are a widespread, perhaps even global, trend. Push them a bit further, and they will affirm that social media are genuinely significant somehow, but they might have a hard time pinning down exactly how or why. If you probe deeper yet and ask them if or how social media will transform the way businesses work, most people won't have a clear answer at all. This is entirely understandable, given that the digital world has virtually remade the means and tools of digital communication in just a few years.

Keeping track of changes and catching up to the pace of change has been hard for even the most dogged marketing manager, product engineer, customer care lead, information technology manager, or C-level executive. As a recipe for making operations difficult for businesses to effectively engage their customers, workers, and the broader market in the new digital landscape, it's almost a perfect storm. Fortunately, it no longer has to be this way. As the understanding of the changes in our pervasively networked, digital world grows, we believe that organizations can, by design, make their way into the future by incorporating the powerful new ways of working that social media represent deeply into the primary functions of their business.

The shift to social media is happening all around us every day. A broad demographic change in the way that people connect and communicate, as well as work and live together, began in the mid-2000s. The change has been labeled with many names: *social networking, Enterprise 2.0, crowdsourcing, customer community, social media marketing,* and any of the other catchphrases that we explore in this book. Because of social media's different way of getting results, the exact nature of changes that they cause in businesses, organizations, government, and even our personal lives has sometimes been hard to pin down. However, they can be much more precisely and elegantly defined than even a couple of years ago. What's more, the key operating principles of social media can be synthesized into simple, easy-to-understand tenets to apply to work. These tenets are presented here for the first time.

In this book, we show exactly why and how organizations must change to survive. Among the many reasons are better financial performance, improved competitive positioning, and long-term sustainability. But accepting the importance of social media is no longer an act of faith: we lay out clear evidence in the chapters that follow that social media are not only transformational to most aspects of enterprises, but also truly better, higher-performing new ways of doing business. In Parts One and Two, we present cutting-edge data matched with eye-opening examples that show how social media, when applied to the way we work, are becoming something known as "social business."

There is occasionally concern in some quarters that social media are technology-driven phenomena and that primarily technology-oriented companies are best at adopting the new digital ways of working. The evidence here shows that this worry is overblown: virtually all organizations can access the benefits of social business, and although some of the early examples we present here are from technology companies that blazed trails, many of the best examples come from those that are as far from the technology industry as can be imagined such as consumer packaged goods company Procter & Gamble and MillerCoors, the well-known beverage conglomerate.

What then do organizations need to understand in order to begin the process of becoming a social business by design? We think it's a clear appreciation of the basic ideas, distilled in a way that's eminently comprehensible. Distributed across the first ten chapters are the clearest declaration yet of what social business fundamentally consists of, collected and organized here as ten core tenets of social business. Studying, understanding, and absorbing these ideas, designed to be approachable by anyone in the business world, free from tools, technologies, or situation, must be the objective of anyone who intends to deeply understand the subject and drive social business transformation in their organization.

GETTING TO SOCIAL BUSINESS

We have been fortunate enough to have seen and helped many organizations start down the road of social business, and the journey certainly can be long and arduous. Yet it's also often highly rewarding. The biggest obstacle is the encouragement and realization of real change. The hard-won lesson is that becoming a social business requires cultural, operational, and technology changes. Of the three, the first two are by far the most time-consuming and challenging to realize, although all three require sustained, conscientious effort. Yet the examples in this book make clear that the same set of strategic changes needs to be made by all companies, even as organizations often discover they already have dozens—and sometimes hundreds—of individual social media efforts, large and small, each trying to drive the same type of transformation.

Many organizations have begun centralizing their efforts, organizing at a high level around many of the thorniest and most difficult aspects, while allowing everyone in the organization to become a social businessperson. Parts One and Two of this book lay out the strongest possible case that organizations must begin the process of moving to social business; Part Three then explores how to make it happen functionally and throughout the enterprise. Getting to social business is a deliberate, conscious process—at least for now. It's also the core idea behind this book. More and more businesses want to get there, but encouraging and enabling is really all they can do. The rest is up to the universe of participants, and that's where the story gets most interesting.

Organizations that want to take the shortest route to becoming social businesses can arm themselves with the data, examples, and approaches we present in this book, which are distilled in an actionable way as never before. We hope that your social business will become a highly successful organization that you codesign with the world.

PART ONE

ADAPTING ORGANIZATIONS TO THE TWENTY-FIRST CENTURY

Chapter 1

Social Media

Drivers of Global Business Opportunity

For German software giant SAP, the road toward social business started, as so many other business success stories have, with a problem. Beginning in the early 2000s, as the firm grew by leaps and bounds, acquiring companies and developing major new versions of its products, it encountered steadily increasing challenges in the ways it provided its vast network of global prospects with information and customers with vital support services and customer care. Although SAP used what were commonly accepted customer support channels such as e-mail and phone, customers were not satisfied with the timeliness or usefulness of the support they received from the company. Another barrier to growth was that prospects were having trouble determining if SAP's complex software solutions would meet their needs.

As SAP's powerful products became more complex and sophisticated, communication issues proliferated. The support needs of over 170,000 customers continued to increase, particularly in key technical areas and with new products. Clearly this issue was having a growing impact on the organization's revenue and growth. SAP's leaders realized something had to be done soon—but what? As they studied the problem, a group of managers determined that any focus on traditional communication channels would drive only minimal incremental improvement. For example, adding more staff to existing support channels had slowed but not entirely mitigated the growing customer relationship issues. SAP reached the conclusion that innovative changes, almost certainly completely new and even untried, were necessary to ameliorate the situation.

To succeed, SAP would have to devise an entirely new way to communicate with and support its customers and prospects. Whatever form a workable solution took, it would have to be able to scale rapidly on a worldwide level, be highly cost efficient, and have a meaningful and sustained business impact on customer relationships.

At the time, online communities were an emerging tool for connecting with and engaging people on topics of mutual interest. These communities were increasingly popular in the consumer world, but most businesses had little expertise or interest in figuring out how they could also drive business results. Intriguingly, online forums were proving particularly effective at organizing far-flung groups of people around common challenges, especially in the area of technology. At the turn of the millennium, the open source software community had become startlingly successful at using closely knit online communities, based on early forms of social media, to create some impressive group outcomes. Entire functioning software products had been completely designed, developed, and supported from thousands of individual contributions made entirely within the online community.

Although online communities demonstrated utility in the software industry, the business models of open source and SAP are vastly divergent. Nevertheless, SAP was intrigued by the possibility of applying new concepts to its service issues. Could the open, shared back-and-forth of online communities deliver significant improvements to customer relationships? SAP had the resources and motivation to research the issue. In 2003, it launched an early form of what eventually became the SAP Community Network, an online community of SAP customers and stakeholders. The goal was to enlist customers and other interested parties to come together online and share ideas and solve problems. In this way, SAP could engage and mobilize the people who were smartest about using its products in the field. Customers could then work together directly and exchange valuable knowledge.

SAP noticed other companies conducting similar experiments with online communities, such as Microsoft's Developer Network, but few of these efforts could be considered large-scale successes. Consequently, far from being a definitive solution to SAP's challenges, it was an experiment, albeit one the company took seriously and made a genuine investment in. Mark Finnern, who went on to become an SAP community evangelist (a formally recognized ombudsman and champion of the service), said of the early days of the SAP Community Network: "To make it work, we knew we'd have to put the people in our company on the front line before customers would engage. It would be 90% us and 10% them at first. But we knew if we did that, it would eventually be 10% us and 90% them."[1] This required a substantial commitment of employee time across the company, but it was essential in helping kick-start participation by customers and partners.

Initially the online community was aimed at software developers from among SAP's customers and business partners who had intensive support and information needs involving SAP's products. SAP experts engaged with customers in the network, which greatly enriched the community because customers often had just as timely and useful hands-on experience as company representatives did. It wasn't long before customers began relying on the community to get key information: more than 100,000 individuals joined within the first two years. By plugging customers into the process of creating reusable knowledge, every contribution made both SAP and the community much richer and more useful. What's more, the process was repeatable, scalable, and relatively inexpensive compared to traditional customer support methods.

Eight years after its founding, the SAP Community Network consists of over 2.5 million registered users and is a vibrant hub and primary support vehicle for a wide range of SAP product lines (Figure 1.1). Benefits center around reduced support costs, driven

TODAY
· 1.5M UMV
· +100K CONTRIBUTORS/YR
· +1M NEWSLETTER SUBS
· SAP IDEA PLACE LAUNCHES

2011

CODE EXCHANGE
LAUNCHES

2010

ECOHUB APP
STORE LAUNCHES

CAREER CENTER
LAUNCHES

2009

BUSINESS OBJECTS
COMMUNITY LAUNCHES

UNIVERSITY ALLIANCES
COMMUNITY LAUNCHES

2008

REBRANDS AS SCM

1M MEMBERS

2007

BPX LAUNCHES

2006

1M FORUM POSTS

2005

100K MEMBERS

FORUMS, BLOGS LAUNCH

2004

SAP DEVELOPER
NETWORK LAUNCHES

2003

Figure 1.1   History of the SAP Community Network

Note: UMV = unique monthly visitors; SCM = SAP community members; BPX = business process expert community. Ecohub is the name of the brand for one of SAP's app stores for partner products. *Source:* SAP AG.

by community sourcing of solutions to customer problems, with high-quality information delivered in a timely fashion to customers and prospects. The collective wisdom of the SAP Community Network (SCN) is now used around the clock to solve customer problems, with over 250,000 community members contributing to the knowledge base.[2]

SAP regards the SCN as a strategic asset, describing it as a professional social network that drives tangible benefits for both the company and its customers. These benefits address the heart of the original problem: how to reach and assist customers and prospects better. SAP cites SCN for improving customer retention, creating efficiency, and driving top-line growth and revenue.[3] Other companies have since gone on to create similar social relationships with customers, but few have been as successful as SAP or have turned it into such an essential component of their business as a sustained competitive advantage.

USING SOCIAL MEDIA STRATEGICALLY FOR HIGH-IMPACT BUSINESS OUTCOMES

SAP's story is an important one in what the world is increasingly calling *social business*—the intentional use of social media to drive meaningful, strategic business outcomes. As we will show throughout this book, social media can be used for significant, sustainable transformative value creation. By intentionally designing new social business models with customers, employees, and value chain partners, any forward-thinking organization can direct and guide social business efforts to access the very highest level of mutual value creation.

Until quite recently, social media were viewed either as a consumer activity, with marketing as the most useful activity for businesses to be engaged in, or something workers used inside the company to collaborate, and occasionally for product innovation or customer care. However, social media have now infiltrated practically every aspect of business operations, and perspectives have expanded

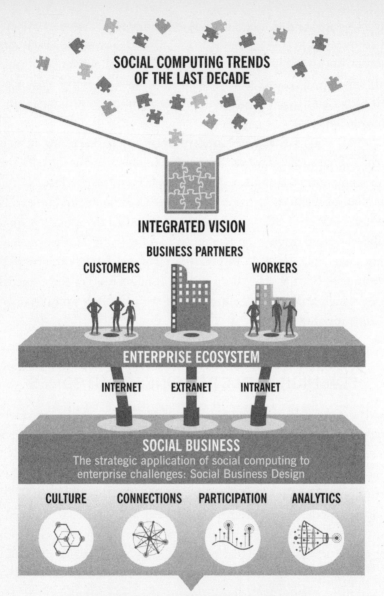

Result: High value, high scale, cost effective, and emergent business outcomes

Figure 1.2   The Social Business Marketplace Continuum: Customers, Business Partners, and Workers

to consider four major and interrelated audiences combined with all types of business activities: customers, the marketplace, workers, and trading partners (see Figure 1.2).

Most businesses will seek to update existing work streams and functions with social activities as nondisruptively as possible. However, simply adding a few social media features to a business activity isn't going to have nearly the impact as carefully and intentionally designed improvements. Fortunately, a number of companies have been able to achieve overhauls of their existing business processes and generate significant benefits.

APPLYING SOCIAL BUSINESS TRANSFORMATION TO EXISTING BUSINESS FUNCTIONS

Seattle-based software giant Microsoft had been in a holding pattern, struggling with the doldrums of corporate middle age. The company had a growing challenge supporting its vast network of over 180,000 software development and value-added reseller partners. Its partner network had been its strategic advantage in the software industry since at least the mid-1990s, providing an ability to quickly dispatch consulting experts to customers and prospects across a wide range of vertical industries.[4] Microsoft created a flow of new business for partners that delivered tailored, product-specific consulting, while partners helped ensure that customers used the full benefits of Microsoft products with long-term loyalty to the company's solutions.

However, as the partner program continued to grow and diversify, its size made it difficult for Microsoft to support and engage effectively using traditional means. Worried about the state of affairs, a survey of the partners in 2009 confirmed Microsoft's worst fears: 64 percent of partners were less than satisfied with the software company. Just as damaging, the survey revealed global partners' perception that Microsoft didn't value them and provided only a bare minimum of proactive communication, such as periodic formal e-mail announcements and occasional online updates—62 percent of partners expressed a strong desire for improved support and information.

Microsoft executives concluded that bold action was necessary to avoid losing the vaunted partner relationships that had been instrumental in making the Fortune 500 leader an industry juggernaut. A key insight in their analysis was that existing channels of communication had lost their effectiveness as collaboration expectations between Microsoft and its partners had risen. In response, Microsoft decided to use the same social media tools that had been effective in helping people organize quickly and effectively elsewhere in the world. Microsoft began an integrated effort to employ Twitter and launch new blogs, publishing in languages specific to the locales where they needed to reengage partners, increasing the flow of vital information, and fostering increased participation. This meant the company effectively employed a reverse version of strategy that citizens had been using to drive governmental regime change. But rather than individuals organizing to topple an institution, in this case the institution was organizing to unite with its diversified constituent base.

Within a few months, Microsoft's continuous read-and-respond strategy, consisting of close monitoring of relevant social media conversations with a matching reply in short time windows, began to turn the situation around. In the first year of the new social media engagement program, partner satisfaction levels increased by double digits to 15 percent. Microsoft experienced even better results in the program's second year, with a 17 percent increase in overall partner satisfaction. Over the same time period, a 30 percent corresponding drop in calls to the company for partner assistance provided a key cross-check that the partner program was actually turning around.[5]

It might come as little surprise that Microsoft and SAP, technology companies, have been fairly adept at applying social technology to their businesses. However, many social business transformation stories exist outside the technology industry. In fact, one of the best examples of rethinking an existing business process comes from the fast-moving consumer goods industry. Consumer products multinational Procter & Gamble found itself in a market situation similar to Microsoft's: a core product line supported by tried, true, and tired communication tactics. Old Spice, one of its best-known products, was a customer favorite but losing market share, especially among younger consumers, to new competitors. In response, Old Spice rolled out advertising slogans such as, "The original. If your grandfather hadn't worn it, you wouldn't exist," which did little to increase sales.

The brand management team realized that revitalizing the brand required more than new slogans generated by advertising. It came up with an idea that would use traditional media but integrated heavily with social media support. The new campaign presented an updated image for the product showcased by actor Isaiah Mustafa. New advertisements for Old Spice launched during the 2010 Super Bowl and the television commercials were posted on YouTube, with the @OldSpice Twitter account engaging with consumers in real time. When individuals tweeted the "Old Spice guy," Mustafa responded in YouTube videos, even referencing the tweets, engaging everyone from celebrities and influencers to everyday people. This type of real-time response in advertising was unheard of. Whereas ads typically take weeks to produce, shoot, and publish, Old Spice was creating new ads in hours, with a copywriter standing by ready to respond to tweets and video comments, an actor with a warehouse full of props like faux Olympic medals, and media channels that enabled rapid publishing and instant feedback.

The wide reach across traditional media kick-started social media participation, which then led to compelling two-way conversations in social media between Old Spice and consumers. Together they created a groundswell of response in the marketplace, with one estimate that the combined campaign reached nearly half of the Internet over its lifetime. The engagement numbers are impressive: on the first day, the social marketing campaign received almost

6 million views, more than President-Elect Obama's victory speech, which received nearly 5 million views. The social media campaign eventually went on to achieve 1.4 billion views after six months.[6] However, as significant as these numbers are, it's the bottom-line results that should make business leaders sit up and take notice.

After years of declining sales and decreasing relevance for Old Spice, the new campaign helped increase sales of the product by 27 percent after just six months, a growth rate that continued to accelerate, showing 55 percent after three months and 107 percent in the month following the engaging campaign. More significant, Old Spice went on to become the top body wash brand for men, something that would not have been the case without the well-integrated traditional and social media aspects of the marketing effort. These exemplary results and significant return on investment serve as a good example of what's possible when redesigning an existing business function to be more social.[7]

Once purely a consumer phenomenon and used only by businesses for limited purposes, social media are now achieving increasingly serious business results. Early and recent adopters are realizing benefits and strategic outcomes far beyond minor increases in productivity and efficiency; they are driving significant changes in unleashed creativity and productive output with very different cost structures and investment levels than traditional business methods. In the next chapter, we begin looking at the trends that contribute to social business.

Chapter 2

Social Media

A Way of Life, a Way of Business

Businesses are learning to apply social media strategically for significant and meaningful outcomes: driving revenue and sales growth, improved customer relationships, superior and highly innovative new products, and higher levels of efficiency and productivity.[1]

The stories in Chapter One and hundreds of others in society, business, and government—some of the most illustrative of which we explore in detail in this book—now herald the arrival of a fundamentally new form of individual power. Aided by new online technologies that enable enormous global influence at very little cost to individual actors, this new power drives collective self-determination and growing decentralization of institutions and businesses. This power shift from classical bastions of power—economic, political, cultural, and otherwise—in favor of loosely organized communities of individuals has been at least two decades in the making, since Tim Berners-Lee created the World Wide Web as we know it in August 1991.

The inflection point was during the rise of popular new global social networks starting in 2007 that made the shift readily apparent to casual observers: increasingly people were choosing simpler, more natural, and open forms of communication based on something now recognized as social media, a collective form of online participation that is not controlled by any person or organization. Social media made it extremely easy to connect with almost any other individual in the world: student, celebrity, politician, athlete, or just another businessperson. Anyone could quickly and easily communicate, share knowledge, or jointly accomplish just about any common activity. Ready access to social media combined with widespread adoption in most developed nations has now almost completely eliminated the barrier for individuals around the world to come together, rally around, and actualize the ideas that matter to them most.

The consequence of such global social networking and widespread adoption of other social media—as of 2012, an estimated 1 billion people use them (Figure 2.1)—is that we have entered an age of individual empowerment the likes of which has not been seen since the widespread introduction of the printed word.[2] A stream of highly accessible and virtually free technologies—this includes social media but also other novel methods of organizing like crowdsourcing—are transforming empowerment far beyond basic sentiment. They are putting vast, world-changing power into the hands of anyone that would use them.

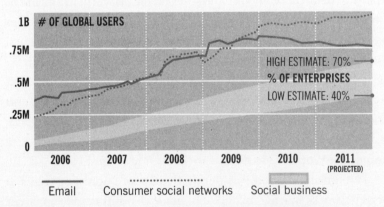

Figure 2.1 The Rise of Social Media and Social Business

Sources: comScore, Hitwise, The Radicati Group, Forrester, APC, Intellicom, Nielsen Norman Group, Social Business Council, NetStrategy/JMC.

To some, these trends and statements might sound like high-minded concepts that won't have much impact on the day-to-day activities of the organizations that comprise our economies and political systems. However, businesses and bureaucracies have been in the direct path of this social revolution as individuals around the world exert their newly found influence. Increasingly those in the developed—and now the developing—world are beginning to sense their ability to drive the changes that matter to them and that they would like to see realized in business, government, and other areas. In the vast virtual halls of the social world, consumers are engaging with each other, demanding respect, organizing, and making those who are traditionally used to one-way flows of control and power take notice and listen to them.

Like any other double-edged sword, empowerment can be employed to just about any end. The infamous Tottenham-sparked riots across London in 2011, for example, covered an entire spectrum of ways in which social media can be employed, for positive outcomes and otherwise. The rioters used social media to organize chaos on the ground as well as criminal activities. But social media also were used subsequently to identify perpetrators and coordinate the cleanup of the aftermath. Fortunately, the users of this new form of social power typically aren't sharing government secrets, overthrowing tyrants, or inciting riots. They are ordinary people who are rapidly understanding the nature of the growing power in their hands. More and more today, an organization's or government's perceived measure of authenticity, authority, fairness, trust, and good faith won't last long when the fundamental yardstick of influence is measured in real time by these very traits. Those without them will be ignored or, worse, will experience a profound loss of control over their customers, markets, and even their products and services. While this may seem alarmist wording at first reading, some of the case studies we present in this book make a strong case for the deeply disruptive yet simultaneously opportunity-rich nature of social business. Nevertheless, thus far, the transitions to social business have largely been nondisruptive.

Social business is one of the biggest shifts in the structure and process of our organizations in business history. It taps into entirely new sources of creative output (everyone on the network), relinquishes structure that reduces productive outputs, and inverts methods of traditional control and decision making in work processes (anyone can contribute as long as they create value) while focusing on useful outcomes.

As a result, there's a growing sense in some parts of the business community that traditional power and control will have a hard time continuing in their existing forms. Influential business thinker and strategist JP Rangaswami has been exhorting businesses for several years to begin "designing for loss of control" based on his experiences as chief information officer of British Telecom, one of the largest organizations in the world.[3] Influence and power are inexorably flowing into everyone's hands now that all individuals have access to equally powerful tools for self-expression. Examples include user-generated media, where over sixty hours of video are uploaded to YouTube every minute, and open source software, designed by volunteers and now the leading source of software in the world. Every company now has to consider virtual competition with the entire world, not just a few large businesses, as competitors evolve faster and possess better tools, technologies, information, and methods of organization than ever before.

As we'll see throughout this book, the future of business is turning into a very different one from what it was in the twentieth century. Institutions unwilling to respond in kind with the new sensibilities and types of engagement the marketplace wants and increasingly expects will experience the consequences. For those that don't, customers and employees will soon come to distrust them, with consequences that vary but inevitably will be undesirable. Today customers who want to use a company's products can quickly consult with the collective experience of the world or broadcast their disapproval of the outcome globally for all to see. Prospective workers no longer have to take a company's assurance of what employment will be like; they can rapidly find out from people who already work there. But this new world is far from the exclusive benefit to consumers; businesses too can benefit. They can now pick and choose new partners in an open marketplace, where business reputations and prior performance are shared and visible for all to see.

To sum up the impact of all of these changes, new social models and enabling tools, combined with the means to employ them effectively, are remaking the landscape of business, society, culture, and government. This future can appear to be daunting, uncertain, and decidedly unfamiliar. But more and more, companies are studying what's happening, absorbing the lessons to be learned, and gaining competency in what's required to succeed in this new world. Even better, there are now numerous stories of large companies that have been successful in their journey to become genuine social businesses.

Success stories of early adopters and movers and shakers are emerging in this brave new period of social business. Fortunately, our collective understanding of the mechanisms is far enough along to understand the broad outlines of what social business entails. The principles of social business are surprisingly simple and straightforward. Virtually every significant outcome we cover in this book is based on three essential concepts. It's primarily due to their simplicity that social business is so powerful and effective at creating sustained results for those who employ the ideas in meaningful way. Wielding them successfully in an organization, however, requires a considerable change in the way we think about business and how it gets done.

The fundamental principles of social business can be distilled down to three basic ideas.

Social Business Tenet #1
Anyone can participate.

The processes of product development, marketing, sales, operations, customer support—in short, nearly all aspects of business—will ultimately be open, social, and participative. This applies to employees, business partners, customers, and the rest of the world and includes all possible uses. Although there must be some constraints and rules regarding who gets to participate and when, in general, the more open the participation, the more superior the result. When people and their friends use the explicit connections they have between each other, participation is most vibrant and useful.

Social Business Tenet #2
Create shared value by default.

Contributors have intrinsic worth based on their inherent ability to increase overall community value through participation. Building value requires that whenever possible, contributors automatically share content with the entire community in as close to real time as possible. The individual reputations of contributors matter as well, along with the resonance of their contribution with others engaged in similar work to create a virtuous participation cycle. Most shared value is created in simple social connection and incremental contributions such as conversations; however, contributions can be complex and sophisticated as well. Individual additions of shared value are tiny, but when they are aggregated into the output of millions of customers and interested stakeholders, value builds exponentially and accumulates into industry-leading outcomes. Formally, the process of automatically building shared value is called a *network effect*.

Social Business Tenet #3
While participation is self-organizing, the focus is on business outcomes.

Control in social business is ultimately embodied in those willing to participate or contribute. This can be through information, financial support, or access to expertise. It can be by anything of worth, though it's typically by the intrinsic value of the contribution alone. Although businesses can be uncomfortable with this fact at first, the control processes of social business are often not well defined. They can and will change dynamically based on the community that drives it. What separates this approach from that of consumer social media (as opposed to social business) is that while social media use the same processes and tools, the goals are solely those of the individuals. In social business, it's specifically about productive shared outcomes for all involved, as well as the business objectives the organization has for its participation. This tenet requires social media to be put to good business use, even though many other outcomes will result as well.

Sounds simple, right? Perhaps too simple and naive to produce serious business outcomes? At first glance, it seems to be a complete departure from the familiar hierarchical command-and-control processes of most businesses today. Consequently it's not uncommon for those encountering these social business ideas to demand immediate answers by business leaders to some tough questions: How can work productively get done with such open and seemingly uncontrolled processes? How does a business maintain direction, focus, control, and ownership of the results? What are the business models, and how does a social business generate revenue?

The ability to apply social business seems to work best in social media, though it's not required (social business ideas can work in many other contexts as well, such as e-mail, in-person work activities, or even executive leadership). In practice, the actors are identified very clearly—often through a user profile or other strong identification mechanism—and their activities are public and tied directly to this identity. This is a powerful accountability mechanism as well as a way to ensure proper credit and sourcing for contributions. Social networks, a popular form of social media, are grounded in identity and activity-tracking mechanisms that end up causing the three essential tenets to work simply and easily to produce surprisingly effective and robust business outcomes.

In the next chapter, we look more deeply at how to address these questions by providing examples of some organizations that have had success applying the three tenets. Because truth grounded in these fast-moving global charges is essential, we explore the stories of those who are directly on the front lines of social business. And we show some intriguing answers that we have discovered to these key issues.

Chapter 3

Who's Winning in Social Business and Why

Those who are looking at social business for the first time through the lens of how they do things now often have difficulty seeing how it could be a repeatable and reliable way of working, much less that it would be effective. However, social business tenets diligently applied throughout the organization become useful and yield transformative results. Unlike the early days of social media, results are not the problem; managing the richness and sheer scale of outcomes presents the greater business challenge. Not only will organizations that engage in social business be able to achieve dramatic improvements in output and productivity, they will generally reap rewards that will be almost too numerous to count. The riches include superior innovation, lower defect rates, cost reductions, higher quality, faster market response, and more. In exchange, organizations must change how they work and move beyond their current assumptions that determine how goals are met, what work is done, and where value comes from.

The performance benefits of social business have been the subject of thorough study and analysis by some of the world's leading management organizations. For example, in December 2010 the respected management consultancy McKinsey & Company released the remarkable results of a detailed statistical analysis of companies engaging in various types of social business activities: firms that engaged more systematically in social business processes and approaches had 24 percent higher revenue (see Figure 3.1).[1] Consulting firm Frost and Sullivan has confirmed similar results in its own studies, showing companies that deployed social tools saw improved performance in innovation (68 percent versus 39 percent that didn't deploy), sales growth (76 percent versus 50 percent that didn't deploy), and profit growth (71 percent versus 45 percent that didn't deploy). The numbers are quite impressive and consistent across the board.[2]

Despite this proof of success, issues of control, trust, and risk continue to dominate the social business discussion in most large organizations. However, the aspect that makes companies so uncomfortable—opening up their processes widely to participation from all constituents through social media—nearly always makes those business activities far richer, more relevant, and more cost-effective. Organizations that engage fully in social business can routinely see order-of-magnitude increases in output or reduction in capital expenditure. These seemingly incredible results are possible because they're not incremental improvements but a fundamental rethinking of the way we operate our businesses, how we engage in work, and how to create, harness, and curate shared and open business activity into actionable value. In particular, the notion of curation is an important and vital social business activity that describes how those engaging in social media evaluate, select, and recommend the content and knowledge they encounter and that resonates with them. This recognition of particularly interesting or valuable contributions lies at the core of building shared value and community in online systems.

At this point, you may be thinking that if social business could routinely create results this impressive and repeatable, it would be the top story in every issue of *Harvard Business Review* or *Forbes*. In fact, that's exactly what has been happening, though in incremental pieces

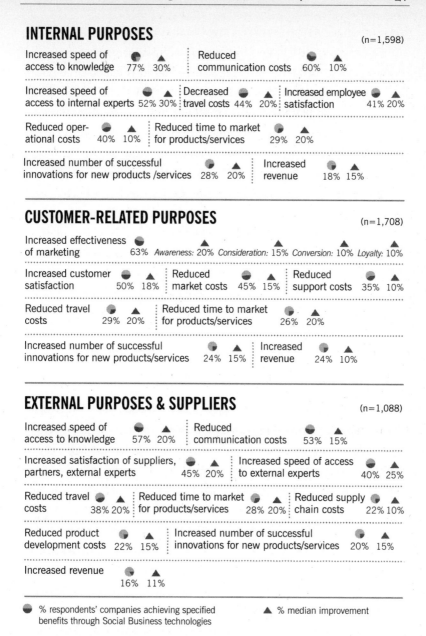

Figure 3.1 McKinsey's Reported Benefits of Social Business

Source: McKinsey & Company.

that often fail to see the big picture, break through the noise, or tell a complete and compelling narrative. The business world's transition to more social and participative business methods is a complex story. The challenge is to look at what the methods of social business offer through a strategic lens that illuminates the full potential of outcomes, laid out in a way that lets businesses systemically activate the methods. Fortunately, most organizations can now rely on the lessons learned by hundreds of companies that have gone before them.

Proof lies with evidence and our understanding of what early adopters have achieved by these methods. In this chapter we take a look at representative stories that show how social business methods work and extrapolate the next level of detail that allows us to begin assembling a rigorous framework that can then be applied to most businesses, large and small, in a repeatable, reliable fashion.

THE SOCIAL BUSINESS WORKPLACE: MILLERCOORS

In the summer of 2010, an executive at MillerCoors, one of the world's largest brewing companies with $7.5 billion in revenue and eighty-five hundred employees, noticed a disturbing trend: female sales executives were departing the company at a much higher rate than their male counterparts. The gender ratio of employees across the company was becoming a concern too, with about a quarter of workers being female compared to 48 percent for the Fortune 100 as a whole. The company wanted to be representative of the best talent and of the marketplace, but with such an imbalance, the challenge was a large one.

MillerCoors started by investigating the root causes of its growing gender imbalance. Focusing on the loss of female sales executives as the most urgent issue, the company discovered that working alone was too isolating for some women, and others, parents in particular, were having trouble with the unpredictable hours that required participating in team and customer meetings at night or even on weekends.

With this information, the company turned to social networking technology designed especially for businesses as a solution to connect workers, provide mutual peer support, and form the basis of an innovative and comprehensive mentoring program designed to retain and help address the needs of top employees. In October 2010, MillerCoors initiated the Women of Sales mentoring program.[3] Forty-five female sales representatives were divided into three groups of fifteen each. Each group was assigned two mentors, either female executives or other leaders from within the company.

Members of each group participated in a private social network to form peer relationships and generate discussion topics, such as sales tactics, personal branding, and work/life balance. They also shared documents or articles pertaining to their discussion threads. The result was an immediate decrease in the rate of attrition. The social tools had enabled connections that were difficult to establish with previous methods, and most of the executives reported that they learned a great deal from their peers that they wouldn't have otherwise.

MillerCoors shows a key lesson in social business: virtual connections drive real-life results. Making it easier to find and connect with coworkers built a sense of community and cohesion that had been lost in a highly mobile and physically fragmented workforce. Social engagement breaks down the isolation that remote workers in large, geographically dispersed companies experience. In addition, the people-oriented connections of social business, although enabled by technology, are very real and can be as effective as in-person relationships.

This lesson appears again and again in social business stories: decentralized, peer-created value assisted by centralized, dedicated resources at headquarters. And it illustrates tenets 1 and 2 of social business: anyone can contribute, and those contributions can and should be designed to increase the value of the entire community.

OPTIMIZING SUPPLY CHAINS WITH SOCIAL BUSINESS: TEVA CANADA

In summer 2011, Teva Canada, a large pharmaceutical firm, publicly reported that it had achieved an unheard-of level of orders fulfilled on time: an impressive 95 percent. It also claimed its manufacturing cycle time had been cut in half, to an average of less than forty days.[4] Teva achieved this high level of operational accomplishment because of a key acquisition the year before: Ratiopharm, a German pharmaceutical company. The new firm brought with it some novel supply chain management methods that employed social media to resolve a set of long-standing supply chain issues.

A few years prior to being acquired, Ratiopharm vice president for supply chain Antonio Martins, facing continued challenges in improving the performance of its supply chain, decided to introduce new collaborative tools to the company's operations center. It began as an experiment that started with a well-known enterprise collaboration tool, Microsoft SharePoint. Martins then added another tool, Strategy-Nets, and finally incorporated a third, Moxie, to fine-tune the outcome. The resulting mix of ad hoc and social media–based collaboration tools, situated within business processes that previously did not have either enough information about what was happening in the supply chain or rapid enough flow of on-the-ground knowledge, ended up resolving many long-standing communication problems. The result of applying open and free-flowing tools of social media to previously information-starved business processes ultimately improved Ratiofarm's internal operations and almost completely fixed its recurring supply chain problems.

Initially Ratiopharm provided workers in the supply chain with a collaborative environment based on SharePoint. Anyone who experienced operations problems would post a description of those problems immediately to the social environment for all to see. Other employees in the supply chain would see the problem report and could reply with solutions and troubleshoot in near real-time. This produced the combined benefit of providing supply chain workers with a matching problem-and-solution notification system, one that had a fast-response loop and rapid, effective access to a wider range of internal experts than they had before.

After this social business process was introduced, the three-month average reaction time to manufacturing interruptions was slashed to two to four weeks. Martins said at the time, "It's easier to get people to chime in on something like a collaboration tool. It's harder to get them to attend and participate in meetings."[5] Connecting people immediately and putting a human face on the work increased engagement with daily activities across the supply chain. It also employed the key social business tenet that anyone can participate in terms of who could report problems and who could solve them.

To improve the efficiency of the social supply chain process even more, Martins selected another solution, Strategy-Nets, to expand collaboration well beyond the supply chain into the marketing, sales, and customer service departments. Connecting supply chain workers to these departments gave managers a better sense of what to expect in terms of orders and product flow and what problems were occurring, and allowed better planning and optimization of business flow. The improved visibility across departments also ensured that customer needs were better met. Martins soon found that the Ratiopharm supply chain now operated more efficiently than he had anticipated.

Once Strategy-Nets was in place, Ratiopharm decided to add the final social component, Moxie, a social tool, enabling real-time conversations and supporting traditional social media such as blogs, wikis, and shared document editing. In this way, a rich tapestry of contributed information was formed around the entire supply chain, as well as other parts of the organization, to fully engage the workforce with social business capabilities.

When Teva acquired Ratiopharm in 2011, the generic drug maker had a service level well below 90 percent and a manufacturing cycle time of approximately eighty days. Once integrated into the parent organization, Martins applied Moxie's collaboration software to Teva's operations, rapidly boosting service levels and lowering manufacturing cycle time. Teva believes, based on the sustained results so far, that further improvements will emerge as workers gain even more experience with the social business environment and refine their use of its capabilities.[6]

As with the MillersCoors story, the fact that anyone could share problems with the supply chain and anyone else could help solve these problems left behind a reusable and growing trail of knowledge aimed at better business outcomes. This story illustrates all three of the tenets of social business and how they generated sustainable success for the organization.

REORGANIZING CORPORATE COMMUNICATION WITH SOCIAL BUSINESS: IBM

IBM remains one of the largest enterprises and well-known brands in the world. With hundreds of thousands of workers in over a hundred countries, IBM has long used emerging communications technologies to connect its employees. In 2009, it realized that the methods and tools it was using were no longer as effective as they once were. As work became more virtual for this technology leader, it was often difficult for workers to keep abreast of what was taking place, find the information they needed, or locate experts in their organization. Customers often felt the same way about IBM.

At the time, the world outside IBM was in the midst of major and generational demographic changes. For the first time in almost two decades, e-mail was no longer the primary way that consumers were staying in touch with each other. In July 2009, the leading Internet traffic measurement firm Comscore reported a sea change: social networks were the primary way that most of the world communicated, eclipsing e-mail for the first time.

Although IBM was not exactly facing an immediate crisis, its response to these changes in the marketplace set it apart from most of its competitors. Seeking to adapt to these new worker and marketplace dynamics, IBM deliberately and systematically reacted to these changes by projecting trends forward and designing new communication approaches, with matching technical capabilities, which were based on where the world of social business was heading. This approach, far more than just dropping powerful new tools into the hands of its workers, was unique for a company of its size.

Once a strategy was in place, IBM deployed its own social business platforms, encouraging workers to use them in addition to public platforms such as Facebook, Twitter, and LinkedIn.

The combined results after several years of social business adoption are impressive. As of 2011, more than 130 communities of IBM professionals around the world were collaborating internally daily using social business tools. Internal research that measures the outcomes of IBM's social business transformation effort has shown a series of benefits: 30 percent reduction in project completion time, 50 percent increased reuse of critical software assets, and an estimated 33 percent reduction in component costs. This does not take into account harder-to-quantify benefits such as increases in employee satisfaction, development of new internal and external relationships, or expertise retention and location. IBM also reported a 29 percent drop in overall e-mail volume during its transition to social business.

IBM has been successful in getting many of its workers to adopt social business activities. As of July 2011 over 25,000 IBM employees were actively using Twitter and 300,000 IBM employees were on LinkedIn, with over 198,000 on Facebook.[7]

As we examine these early adopters, we see that social business organizations that are nimble, driven, willing to experiment at the edges, and push successes toward the center of the organization have important results. IBM's subsequent response to the changing communication landscape was comprehensive and globally coordinated, and it ultimately affected nearly every one of its workers. In 2011, IBM reported that it had successfully become a social business by systematically incorporating new social processes and tools, primarily based on the proven concepts of consumer social media, into the way it engaged with its workers, partners, customers, and ultimately, the whole world.[8]

IMPROVING STOCK TRADES WITH SOCIAL BUSINESS: BLOOMBERG

Financial media and news firm Bloomberg is an extremely competitive data provider for equity trading customers around the world. Since its business relies on having the up-to-the-minute, cutting-edge data, Bloomberg realized that the flow of conversations through social media could provide early insights into market directions. After much research, Bloomberg offered traders social media analysis tools as a real-time sentiment indicator for stocks whose prices closely reflect consumer opinion.

Seeking to put the power of social media insight into the hands of stock traders and equity fund managers, Bloomberg's news and information group partnered with a syndicated data provider, WiseWindow, to use a real-time consumer sentiment analysis technology dubbed Mobi in conjunction with Bloomberg's network of over 300,000 desktop terminals in financial services companies around the world. Mobi's social media analytics technology provided a three-week leading indicator of stock performance in key industry verticals, in addition to a consumer sentiment index for the airline industry and targeted indexes for customer service, pricing, and scheduling. Mobi's use is applicable in many fields and covers a number of key industries, including health care, consumer electronics, and automotive.

Using Mobi, trading firms Derwent Capital and WallStreetBirds mined Twitter chatter for sentiment analysis. They used Mobi's capabilities to scan the Web for consumer opinion across a range of social media such as Facebook and Twitter, online communities, and other likely places where opinions about the companies would be expressed. The intent was to identify, aggregate, and analyze openly shared social media conversations such that the collective activity could be aggregated and then analyzed for positive and negative feelings. Then the results could be directed at business objectives—in this case, whether a stock was going to do well.

The chief executive officer of WiseWindow, Sid Mohasseb, realized the value of looking at the many competing opinions held and expressed in social media: "No single source of online opinions, be it Twitter, Facebook, blogs, etc. is as predictive on its own. Only the aggregate opinions from all sources are truly predictive of an industry's stock prices."[9]

The research that Mohasseb conducted also showed that opinions expressed in social media on specific industry topics are even more predictive than less specific conversation: "Test cases using the automotive industry found opinions about car problems, car quality /reliability/durability and rebates are especially well-correlated with Ford and GM stock prices. Analysis from a top Wall Street investment bank and an independent source confirmed our correlations with weekly automotive sales data." When people talk about companies in social media, the information matches their offline behavior, indicating that social media analysis is particularly effective for business uses like Mobi's correlated market intelligence.

To confirm this, an independent analytics firm, Emerald Logic, conducted a study in 2010 to verify the impact of social media data on equity trading results. The results were remarkable. Patrick Lilley, the firm's chief executive officer, discovered this:

> We tested for the first six months of 2011 on GM, Ford, American Airlines and Southwest Airlines, all of which declined during this period. A simple momentum trading program beat the market, but adding WiseWindow's [social media] data boosted returns by over 30 percent on an annualised basis for GM, Ford, and Southwest Airlines. For American Airlines, the uplift was 65 percent annualised. Volatility of returns was also significantly reduced.[10]

Because of its ability to tap into the collective zeitgeist, social media analytics is quickly advancing to the leading edge of social business. Products like Mobi are making strategic insights available that can change markets, drive profits, and tap into the global brain in a way that's possible only with the open, transparent, and participative channels of social media. That's not to say there aren't challenges and that unscrupulous individuals and organizations won't find ways to influence tools like Mobi. Instead, this story shows an important early success in turning the mass of seemingly unconnected conversations into powerful business tools.[11]

We will examine social business intelligence in more detail, including how to establish it as a potent force for achieving significant new business outcomes similar to what Mobi is accomplishing. To support the case for social business, the three tenets were important in a unique way: by watching everyone's contribution, anyone could be a potential contributor. Broadcast in public social networks, conversations are generally open for all to see, and every contribution can potentially provide value to the Mobi effort, aimed specifically at improving the financial returns of financial industry traders.

BOOSTING RETAILER PRODUCTIVITY WITH SOCIAL BUSINESS: MOUNTAIN EQUIPMENT CO-OP

Mountain Equipment Co-Op (MEC) is a Canadian consumers' cooperative that sells outdoor recreation gear and clothing to its members. Started in 1971, the retail co-op has successfully grown to over 3 million members and counts more than fifteen hundred employees and fourteen retail locations. The workers driving MEC's recent growth hail from a connected and increasingly digital generation who expect to use the same user-friendly tools available in their personal lives in order to communicate with each other at work. Thus, MEC decided to make its existing intranet, the internal Web sites that contain the company's internal information, more social and participative.

Its original intranet, like most other typical corporate intranets, was infrequently updated and information was often out of date, discouraging its use. MEC hoped that opening up the intranet to anyone to add information to share or coordinate with other stores inside the company could improve communication efficiency and raise productivity.

MEC considered its options and selected social intranet tools that were appropriate to its size, mainly a social platform from Thought-Farmer known as Mondo for coordinating schedules, requesting time off, and reordering fresh stock. The company used it for a while and it worked well, but its leaders realized they wanted even more collaboration between staff to tap into the higher level of performance they thought was possible. Once workers' needs and behaviors were better understood, the new social intranet became the home of highly popular and quickly viral forums and interest groups within the company.

The intranet administrators at MEC concluded that the combination of social tools, which encourage communication, and the analysis and resulting customization to encourage useful business outcomes made MEC's intranet much more effective than it was before. Two contributing factors to the outcome stand out: encouragement for all employees to use the intranet and making certain that commonplace communications were open and efficient. Executives found that workers were engaged much more deeply than before, and intranet use has led to rewarding outcomes that they hadn't imagined at the outset.

Most technology professionals have long known that intranets have struggled as centers of communication and collaboration, so MEC was careful to focus improvements on the most frequently occurring and highest-value worker activities. These results, while harder to quantify, were a marked contrast from the sleepy MEC intranet of old. Going from a handful of pages updated each month, users from October to March 2011 alone created over ninety-four hundred intranet pages, contributed seventy-nine hundred discussion comments, and attached thirty-one hundred documents. The results were definitive: engagement on the company's intranet, which had been occasional at best, now averaged 85 percent of all employees.[12]

MEC isn't content to declare victory and continues to make improvements and tweaks to the social features. "We're constantly modifying it," explained Joey Dubuc, the administrator of MEC's new social capabilities. "Your information architecture can always be a little better. We try to figure out what people are using, what they aren't using, and why there aren't using it." MEC found that continuing to adjust the intranet's participative features based on analysis of user participation produced better results.

Businesses can have some challenges getting their social environment started, and MEC was no exception. Initially there was minor difficulty in getting conversations started and useful information flowing in from workers in the new social channels. It was Dubuc who was responsible for monitoring what users did and adapted the new intranet functions to the most productive activities at MEC. By watching how staff members worked day-to-day, he discovered a key strategy for behavior change and better engagement: "People are used to the never-ending pile of email. So it's a cultural shift to go to the site. Once you get a department into using the site and they get the hang of it, it starts to go viral to an extent. It really takes one person to say, 'I saw that on the intranet,' and people get curious about this communication happening on the site instead of email."[13]

Another strategy presented itself as well. Communities have long known that the public actions of its leaders, particularly well-regarded ones, set needed examples of desired behaviors. Dubuc discovered that the same principle applies to communities in social media: "The most important thing was support for Mondo from the top down. Getting senior management involved in the use of Mondo was important for engagement for the rest of the staff. Their online presence encouraged staff to get using the site."

Another problem soon became apparent, however: the people who work in stores like MEC don't spend much of their day on computers, other than a point-of-sale system, making it hard for them to engage in workplace innovations like MEC's social intranet.

Yet these workers have vital knowledge of what's actually taking place in the stores and with customers. MEC intranet designers wanted to find a way to get MEC's staff to use the system efficiently during the day from the stores without taking too much time from their jobs. The solution ended up being simpler than expected: they moved key processes and information, including shift scheduling and vacation requests, frequently used human resource forms, and companywide announcements, to the new social intranet. These seeds then drew in retail workers to the new intranet, provided important work precedents, and fostered new habits, such as engaging with others in the communities they quickly discovered there.[14]

The engagement resulting from these adoption strategies spread to other employees in different cities across the chain. Employees started reading others' profiles and exchanged comments in forums and interest groups, making them familiar with each other. Soon these contacts became trusted sources of knowledge and insight, helping to improve collaboration and efficiency. MEC is particularly proud of its distinctive culture founded on environmental sustainability, close community cooperation, and an abiding passion for the outdoors. These values made the new social intranet even more effective: employees began using it as a way to connect with each about common interests, such as climbing, hiking, camping, and other recreational activities. That these activities were also aligned with the company's purpose made it an even more unifying experience among workers and company leaders and their subsequent work together.

One of the key lessons MEC learned was that successfully encouraging people to move away from e-mail and other productivity applications to an intranet is not a trivial task. Sustained uptake and adoption of the new social intranet were finally achieved by taking a careful, business-focused approach that also took advantage of the company's culture and employee behavior patterns, and then building on early successes when something worked particularly well. Ultimately MEC experienced the same core patterns of social business that recur in all the social business stories presented in this book.

At their root, rewards came to MEC by breaking down the barriers to participation (anyone can contribute), enlisting all workers as sources of valuable knowledge and teamwork (network effects), and focusing on useful business functions. By opening up the intranet to everyone and encouraging them to share their work and interests, MEC finally became a social business.

ENLISTING CUSTOMERS WITH SOCIAL BUSINESS TO CREATE BETTER SUPPORT: INTUIT

In 2007, well-known accounting software services firm Intuit realized that it had a real conundrum on its hands. The company provides tax filing services to millions of customers in North America using self-guided software that replaces the services of a costly expert tax preparer. Known as TurboTax, the software had long been popular for helping tens of millions of people to prepare their tax returns quickly and with minimum hassle.

But TurboTax had a signature challenge: competing with its primary rival and industry leader at the time, H&R Block. By using live workers and maintaining a network of over twelve thousand office locations, H&R Block could provide better support to customers than a software-based solution could. In fact, this was central to the value proposition TurboTax offered to its customers: it was often several times cheaper to use than hiring an expert tax preparer. However, this also meant that when a customer was unsure of how to complete his or her tax return, limited options for obtaining help were available.

Intuit counted on its software being sophisticated enough to assist customers through most of the tax return process. If they needed help, the cost of providing timely support over the phone or by e-mail was prohibitive. Increasingly, given that Intuit could afford a certain level of responsiveness in only its call center in order to compete effectively with the H&R Block and other tax preparers, product abandonment became a real issue. When customers weren't able to get an answer quickly or easily about how to complete their tax returns, they would take their tax returns to a human tax preparer.

After years of ranking as an industry leader, yet second choice compared to traditional tax preparers, Intuit realized it needed to come up with a better way to assist its users than its aging customer support techniques. Given the hard deadlines of tax preparation and tens of millions of users all trying to complete their filing by April 15, packing whole floors of buildings with temporary call center staff armed with knowledge bases wasn't necessarily cost-effective. It also wouldn't scale up if Intuit's products became more popular. Moreover, given that most call center workers were not knowledgeable tax experts, it wasn't likely to give customers what they needed: the best answer possible.[15]

Like SAP and Microsoft, Intuit came to understand that it had to come up with an entirely different way to tackle the problem of supporting its customers in the highly time-sensitive windows right before taxes were due. As more and more companies are realizing as they look at social business solutions, Intuit came to a remarkable conclusion: its single largest and most valuable asset wasn't its brand, its state-of-the-art facilities, or even its thousands of workers. It was its customers. They were the millions who had to file tax returns every year and had been through every possible tax situation.

Perhaps those customers could be used to support other Intuit customers. Intuit looked at a number of options and soon settled on the use of a general-purpose online support community that would allow customers to ask questions and receive replies from Intuit or other customers as needed. This worked well enough but didn't have the impact that Intuit was looking for. It didn't have years to wait for users to learn about the community and populate different subject threads with content. Worse, unlike the sustained customer communities of SAP and Microsoft, the TurboTax product was used only once a year, so people weren't likely to want to spend the time learning how to use the community or invest the effort in becoming members. In the end, these realities made the first attempt at applying social media to Intuit's customer support challenges less successful than its leaders had hoped.

Intuit realized that it needed to make social customer care much easier and more focused on specific support problems. As a result, it created a system called Live Community. Live Community was not a general-purpose discussion forum where people could ask questions in any format, which made it hard to organize and find what customers were looking for. Rather, Live Community was far more focused and transactional. Intuit also took the key step of integrating the Live Community social support experience directly into the TurboTax product itself, which greatly reduced the difficulty in finding the support community and made it easy for anyone to ask a question about a step of the tax return process while in it. And the key to making it work? Intuit also made it possible for anyone to answer any question they saw in the Live Community panel on each screen of the TurboTax product.

How could this work? While some customers might know the answer to a problem, wouldn't a lot of inaccurate answers result? Would enough people actually contribute? More important, could Live Community possibly make enough of a difference to have a substantial impact on Intuit's support challenges?

As it turned out, a social business approach better tailored to Intuit's unique business requirements and its customer-specific needs made a real difference. Live Community quickly proved to be surprisingly effective in providing timely support to customers. Because it wasn't a free-form environment for social chatter and was focused on a specific question-and-answer format, people could quickly access direct answers to their issues. Moreover, it was easy for users to rate answers and remove inaccurate and irrelevant contributions.

Live Community eventually proved to be instrumental to improving customer support and satisfaction. The year after its inception, TurboTax's growth significantly outperformed that of H&R Block, much of it attributable to the better customer support and lower product abandonment due to its innovative and targeted social business support solution.[16] By 2011, Intuit had achieved over twice the market share of its competitor and was becoming the definitive market leader.[17]

By tapping into a much larger source of tax knowledge, allowing open contributions from anyone willing to participate, and making sure those contributions benefited everyone, Intuit was able to scale the support of TurboTax using a far cheaper source of help while also reducing the amount of traditional support it provided. The results of applying social business to customer care had a major competitive impact and changed the complexion of the entire tax preparation industry.

LEARNING TO FOCUS ON WHAT MATTERS IN SOCIAL BUSINESS

The vast, fast-moving arena of social media is a dizzying blend of global and local communities, viral conversations, and a growing array of new social technologies. Services like Facebook, Twitter, and hundreds of new social services appear every year and continuously evolve, add features, and change how they work according to what their users expect from them in a tight feedback loop. Keeping up with it all and extrapolating what works best for the enterprise has become the signature challenge for business leaders and workers alike who seek to benefit from using social media.

However, whether social media are used to energize a marketing campaign, dramatically improve how workers interact and collaborate, or transform how products are developed or customers are supported, the underlying principles remain constant: allow the freest and most open input process the business situation allows, ensure accumulation of value for stakeholders involved to the fullest extent, and ensure that a primary focus of the input process points toward a desired business outcome.

To understand the application of social business ideas, however, we must look at how the world is changing, how social media seem to be directly connected to much of these changes, and how this paints a picture of opportunity for those who wish to apply social business.

Chapter 4

The Global Business Transition to Social Media

The widespread adoption of social media in most of the developed world is a familiar story to most of us and integral to widespread change in society and global culture. To fully understand why, it's necessary to examine the confluence of complex but deeply connected factors that are driving the move to social business:

1. *The growth of the knowledge-based economy* (Figure 4.1). The lion's share of the U.S. labor force has transitioned to service and knowledge work from industry and agriculture. And only knowledge has been growing strongly, with the service sector seeing much slower, although, steady, increases in share as well. As of 2011, over half of the work in developed countries is knowledge work, with some industries, like financial services, having nearly three-quarters of its workforce dedicated to creating and managing high value information. Information is now at the heart of the world economy. Most of this information is kept in computer systems, and a growing amount of it comes from or is kept online.

2. *The widespread availability of free global platforms for self-expression.* As explored in Chapter One, social media are the primary form of communication online, eclipsing e-mail since mid-2009. Other

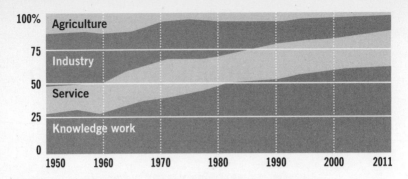

Figure 4.1 The Growth of Knowledge Work, 1959–2011

Source: U.S. Bureau of Economic Analysis, Karl Bening, and other sources.

than the cost to access a computer and the Internet, social media are available for free to the world's population, costing nothing to create and share information within social media that is then immediately accessible around the world. This alone makes it one of the most significant communications revolutions for a number of reasons, including the speed of adoption and the breadth of those affected, currently estimated to be between about half of all Americans and approximately 1 billion people globally.[1] It's also one of the largest single improvements in human history in terms of the ability of people to express themselves and self-organize.

3. *The shift in the bottom-line power of institutions compared to online communities of people.* A curious feature of social networks and online communities is their sheer productive power. At the same time, while businesses are growing larger than ever before, they can't begin to match the scale and creative capability of millions of members of social networks around the globe. Crowdsourcing, the ability to collectively organize a large number of loosely connected people around the world for a common purpose, is just one of the more disruptive possibilities made possible by social media.

4. *Peer production is becoming the primary motivating force for knowledge creation.* Facilitating creation and management of knowledge in

its myriad forms, from movies and stock quotes to software and financial reports, is now a primary activity of the global economy. Social media have removed almost all geographical, economic, and collaborative barriers to creating knowledge. And online communities collectively have more productive capacity than central production processes typically conducted by businesses that hire and pay employees and business partners. Instead, communities of people are able to self-organize and achieve outsized results compared to what companies can achieve on their own.

One particularly potent example of peer production comes from the emerging field of gamification, the use of game mechanics to solve real-life problems. An online community of gamers formed around a new game site created by the University of Washington with the hope that the community could solve a long-standing AIDS protein folding problem that had eluded immunologists for over a decade. Scientists had used the most powerful X-ray crystallography techniques available in order to discern the structure of a particularly difficult protein that was key to unlocking how it evades the body's immune system, but to no avail. The game site, FoldIt, was a last-ditch effort to solve the problem. The results astounded the project's sponsor: a correct resolution to the protein modeling problem in just three weeks. Peer production by amateurs won the day over the dedicated yet small-scale and isolated efforts of teams of experts.[2]

Peer production, both deliberate and unintentional, occurs around the world every day in open source software projects, crowd-sourced marketing research, Wikipedia entries, reviews and ratings on countless e-commerce sites, and, increasingly, highly structured and reusable "off-the-shelf" communities, such as Amazon's Mechanical Turk and Innocentive, commercial services that enable rapid access to already established and thriving communities of people. The former enlists hundreds of thousands of people in simple tasks, and the latter can mobilize communities of scientific and engineering experts

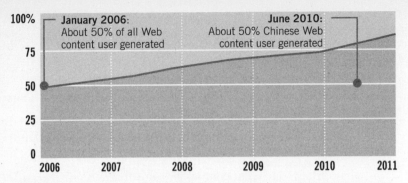

Figure 4.2   The Rise of Peer-Produced Online Content, 2006-2011

Sources: IDC, Forrester, and Data Center of China Internet.

to solve esoteric problems in technical fields. Both are successful services designed as reusable peer production that can be employed easily by virtually any organization. Perhaps most telling of all, most of the Web today is now peer produced, with perhaps the majority being created with social media. (See Figure 4.2.)

In close combination, these four interrelated factors—the growth of the knowledge-based economy, widespread availability of free global platforms, the shift in the bottom-line power of institutions, and peer production as the primary motivating force for knowledge creation—explain at a conceptual level that social media can be transformed into a force for business. This is invaluable for focusing on the major, strategic trends and changes taking place in society and business.

A few key questions should be asked at this point: Does all of the information creation happening in social media result in increases in knowledge? If peer production is suddenly so much easier to engage in than was possible before, is it a repeatable and reliable way to achieve business objectives?

The answers to these questions are critical and go to the heart of the social business hypothesis. While social media have as many motivations for why participants engage, social business is slightly

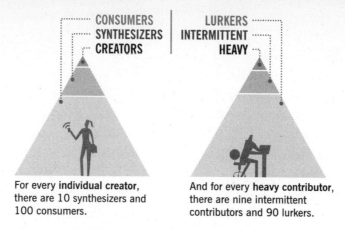

For every **individual creator**, there are 10 synthesizers and 100 consumers.

And for every **heavy contributor**, there are nine intermittent contributors and 90 lurkers.

Figure 4.3 Participation Inequality in Social Media

Source: Horowitz, B. "Creators, Synthesizer, and Consumers." *Elatable*, Feb. 16, 2006. http://blog.elatable.com/2006/02/creators-synthesizers -and-consumers.html.

different. A famous piece of research by Bradley Horowitz, a Google executive and vice president for the Google+ social network, shows that creation is a much less common activity in social media than consumption is.[3] In fact, it breaks down into the interesting pyramid on the left in Figure 4.3, which says that only about 1 percent of a group will be producers, with another 10 percent recombining and synthesizing the resulting work. On the right is well-known intranet researcher Jakob Nielsen's equivalent for participation levels inside businesses for the creation of information.

What all this means is that in any typical social group only a "remarkable 1 percent" will actually create. There are several implications to this. For one, it means that the communities must be very large indeed to outproduce traditional business methods or they must be atypical in their behavior (for example, much more than 1 percent of the community would contribute). In fact, one or both of these can be the case when engaging in social business. Often the engagement process is a broad net across the Internet to gather interesting participants. Or organizations can go directly to communities that specialize in peer production, such as the services like Amazon Mechanical Turk or other special interest communities, many of them noncommercial.

This doesn't answer the question of whether user contributions directly translate into usable knowledge and therefore productive output. As anyone who has used Facebook or Twitter can attest, there's a lot of noise inherent in most social conversation, even when directed at a specific objective. Like the Intuit example of Live Community in Chapter Three, often a general-purpose social media environment is not focused enough. Sometimes it's better to limit the axes of participation enough to constrain output without hindering participation.

Almost all social business efforts that access a focused, reasonably sized community create more usable input than required to meet business needs. This evidence gives us another two tenets of social business that are not quite as core as the first three but deeply inform professionals in applying social business methods:

Social Business Tenet #4
Enlist a large enough community to derive the desired result.

Most social business efforts either engage with an existing community or build their own. The first approach is much easier but may not suffice for the effort. Engaging with an existing community has its own challenges, given that businesses must follow the rules of that community, whereas building a new community around a specific purpose can ensure amenable rules. However, creating a community is much more work and usually requires a large—and typically expensive—funnel to pull in large enough groups of participants and interlocutors. Either way, businesses must have a good means for calculating the size of the community they need to accomplish the business objective, whether it's internal collaboration or external engagement. One counterintuitive outcome of opening up a business activity to anyone, however, is that occasionally participation can far exceed what's needed or expected. Because open processes are far less predictable, they can exceed expectations without warning. Be just as ready for too much as too little participation in planning any social business effort.

Social Business Tenet #5
Engage the right community for the business purpose.

Countless online communities and subcommunities exist in social networks and other platforms. Most are poorly defined or exist in niches surprisingly difficult to locate, connect with, or establish trust within. While tenet 4 is critical for sizing the volume of participation, tenet 5 establishes the need to have alignment with communities being engaged with or created. Alignment comes in many forms and is a demographic and social psychology challenge. To a fairly amazing extent, communities based on social media are very self-selecting. Business activities truly open to participation will attract a surprisingly wide variety of interested stakeholders. Put simply, the community one wants is the community that can deliver on what both the community and the business need.

With five tenets in hand, we have almost enough of a palette to begin designing social businesses. But in order to deliver high-impact results, we have to look at a few more key aspects of the changes taking place in society, business, and technology.

Chapter 5

How Business Will Make the Transition

It's far easier for small and medium-sized companies than large ones to change the way they work. The methods through which they interact and stay connected to the marketplace and their customers are easier to change when there are fewer constraints. In contrast, large companies are challenged when making the transition to social business because they have to deal with change on a large scale. People are the primary element of any successful business transformation, and changing people is notoriously difficult. Thus, the larger the business, the greater the difficulty encountered.

The ongoing and seemingly inexorable decline of a traditional industry such as old media continues to be a canonical example of what happens when the ground rules change in an industry fundamentally unable to adapt to new market conditions. In this chapter, we explore some of the more traditional limitations that virtually all organizations face as they realize they have to literally destroy what are often hallowed processes, traditions, and internal institutions. The resulting so-called new normal has begun to seem more and more foreign than most organizations are willing to accept. The shifts of control required by social business are challenging: how we communicate (from point-to-point to social), how we organize (hierarchies to communities), how we create (central output to peer output), and where value comes from (hierarchies to networks).

The old question about the innovator's dilemma has become more urgent as the new business landscape looks increasingly unfamiliar. We now live in an age when historically scarce resources have become abundantly available in seemingly unlimited quantities: new ideas, existing knowledge, productive capacity, and access to an organization's customers and competitors. Conversely, what was formerly abundant is now scarce: broad demand for big-ticket, high-margin, low-volume products and services in the form of large advertisers, big corporate customers, and anything else. Business has become increasingly finely grained, scaled, and oriented around mass customization as opposed to traditional scaling of one-size-fits-all.

Businesses frequently remain uncomfortable about exploring the future in an uncertain and rapidly changing landscape. The feedback cycles of social media are relentlessly real time, affecting every major business function, though some certainly more than others, particularly marketing, customer care, and human resources. One response that occurs frequently is serious discussion about "putting the genie back into the bottle" and reverting to old models for collaborating on and producing work. One of the most famous examples of this was when newspaper magnate Rupert Murdoch decided to ignore new Internet business models and require that many of his news outlets charge for access to their Web sites, despite the fact that companies like Google were much more successful in monetizing in entirely new ways with advertising and other indirect fees.[1] Industries directly in the firing line of social media, including Hollywood and virtually all media, have been exposed to profound disruption, such as when Amazon decided in 2011 to directly connect authors with its global online publishing network, cutting out publishers and editors altogether.[2]

Responses like these are near-desperate attempts from fading industries deeply affected by changes brought about by the digital revolution. These efforts are usually misguided, shortsighted, and insufficiently imaginative. These periodic debates also show the future of social business and the need for effective vision and transformation.

Old media have felt the impact of social media, and the software industry has been dramatically affected by open source (software peer produced by global communities). Other industries are lining up for similar disruptions, including most industries involved in services and knowledge work that can be recast in social business terms. In the near term, these include financial services, education, information services, consulting, and most administration and government. Over the longer term, social business will transform most human activity. Ultimately everything that can be social will be social.

NEXT-GENERATION BUSINESS: OPEN, SOCIAL, AND SELF-SERVICE

How do businesses cross the divide between the traditional business era and the social business era? An example of how foreign yet novel these new ways of doing business will be is the story of reCAPTCHA, a service that puts brief, hard-to-read text snippets on forms in Web sites so that users can prove that they are really humans and not spammers or bots. The service was designed to process the several hundred million online verification forms that are filled out every day around the Web. The creators of the product soon realized they had unintentionally "created a system that was frittering away, in ten-second increments, millions of hours of a most precious resource: human brain cycles."[3] In response, they pivoted the reCAPTCHA service to tap into a huge reservoir of highly cost-effective labor to tackle enormous problems. Turning individual work into collective productivity, the system started using images from failed optical character recognition (OCR) jobs in its human verification tests (the text displayed is actually scanned from a printed source).

reCAPTCHA subsequently went on to digitize over a century of newspaper and print archives from the *New York Times* and plans to accomplish far more going forward.[4] Businesses that employ OCR correction staff and compete with this service are at primary risk for disruption if they don't change their methods. This seemingly limitless and free source of mental and physical effort (both recognition and keying) has been harnessed by reCAPTCHA at virtually no cost. The service taps into community output—the community of all Web users. reCAPTCHA doesn't actually control its own product; its partners that use its badge do, thereby contributing their users and delivering shared benefit to all involved. This loosely shared cooperative partnering using the network is a simple yet powerful example of the enormous scale and value possible with social business models.

In the social business era, successful organizations will be open to participation, tapping into far-flung communities and social networks to accomplish work on larger scales than they ever imagined. In the process, they must overcome organizational, cultural, structural, legal, and regulatory barriers and rethink how business gets done.

WHAT SOCIAL BUSINESS CONSISTS OF

Emerging new institutions—social businesses—will look very different from most organizations today. They will derive power and value from deep integration into the lives of both the people and businesses they touch on, not from a large centralized market presence. Think of reCAPTCHA as the twenty-first-century organization: deeply networked to millions of partners, highly participative by enlisting millions of participants, and both delivering and providing value in an integrated and profoundly connected way.

A social business consists of three unique and critical aspects:

1. It creates and delivers most of its value over the network, usually indirectly (not centralized production, but peer production).
2. It consists of a loosely coupled entity—usually a very large number of customers and suppliers who have as much control over outcomes as any other part of the business.

3. It has effective strategies to take advantage of the new balance of abundance and scarcity, along with greatly reduced dependencies on the old balance.

Social business models and operating structures are tuned to operate smoothly using the post-Great Recession resource-and-demand landscape.

Self-organizing peer production is the motive force, network effects are the new market share, and social power structures are what drive businesses forward, becoming perpetuating communities of self-interested, like-minded individuals. Figure 5.1 depicts these changes, including the series of major shifts taking place in the consumer and

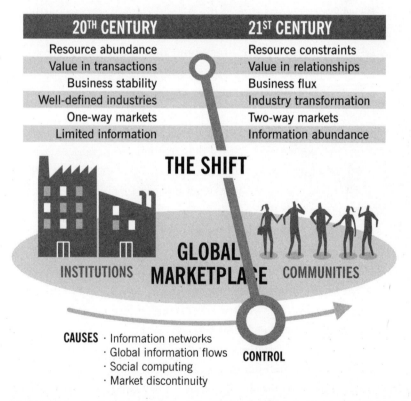

Figure 5.1   Societal and Economic Shifts Leading to Social Business

business landscapes today. The premise is that organizations must begin organizing differently to embrace these trends and remain successful. We believe that operating like a social business is at the core of many of the changes required by companies to thrive today and avoid disruption.

Putting aside for now the legal, societal, and cultural impacts and challenges of all this (barriers explaining why the transformation to social business has taken so long, despite the Internet having existed for decades), let's focus on the business side. The new business landscape will still take a half-decade or more to arrive, and these drivers explain how markets will get there:

- *Strategic control over peer-produced community data drives market dominance.* The irreplaceable value of the social business economy is high-value information. It is the currency of the realm on the network, which will always route to the best source. Only the richest and most up-to-date data sources will have market dominance, and they will have inordinate market power as well. Traditional companies greatly undervalue and underexploit their vast data assets today. In contrast, social businesses can't and don't. They relentlessly use these assets to their advantage as a high-value revenue stream, monetizing it in ways their communities and their own organizations benefit from.

- *Peer production is the most efficient and richest source of value creation.* Centralized production is inefficient and less optimal compared to social business methods. When you can tap into the vast capabilities of the global populace for mutual benefit, delivering it through a central production route is not competitive for most purposes. Networked resources will almost always greatly outnumber whatever classic business processes can bring to bear. The traditional means of enlisting contribution (employment) won't work; something new will be required.

- *Social power structures are the means of self-organizing and governing.* Organizational hierarchy remains in place to set business goals and objectives, but social models are leveraged as effective and efficient ways to run organizations. Work itself, however, takes place through community-based relationships that drive business activities and objectives forward. The commercial and community motivations that have made open source software so successful as a productive model based on social power structures serve as powerful examples of how this is taking place. Many others are presented in this book. With the adoption of social business, a full range of social business models will be involved, from internal social collaboration to customer care communities.

- *Mass self-servicing of market niches achieves the highest economic scale.* Social businesses will use self-service as their primary means of interaction with the market, whether integrating with open data or letting customers and partners distribute their functionality to the far corners of the world. Google's industry-leading AdWords online advertising service is a great example of this, offering incredibly detailed control to a wide spectrum of customer types, all without human intervention on the company side.

- *Cloud- and ecosystem-based open supply chains are the basis of growth and agility.* Social businesses will literally be distributed along the edge of the network in the cloud, becoming both a volume supplier and a consumer of others' best-of-breed services. Social business will build on other best-of-class and trustworthy social companies and noncommercial communities, building a vibrant and deeply meshed supply chain ecosystem while carefully exposing and protecting strategic data.

- *The ability to dynamically adapt and rapidly respond to the current needs of the cloud is vital.* Because of the self-organizing aspect of social media, change will be more rapid and unpredictable than in the past since it will often be led on the community side. People in social business ecosystems will make decisions and change course, affecting businesses and customers much faster than traditional business models do. Success requires designing for low levels of central control and enabling highly fluid evolution and development based on near-real-time market feedback.

HOW SOCIAL BUSINESSES WILL EMERGE

So far we have painted a high-level picture of how the business landscape will become transformed over the next decade or so. However, for some protected and highly regulated industries, it may take longer than expected. There are macrotrends that also affect how social businesses will either emerge from the successful transformations of existing organizations, or grow as successful start-ups. These trends will have a direct impact on how successful an existing organization will be as it tries to become a social business by design:

- *New resource constraints.* Today's economic baselines (the Great Recession, green business models, and peer production, for example) require organizations to find new ways of accomplishing goals using fewer resources. This includes identifying the means to capture opportunity and transform in-process business activities using newer, more efficient models. Social businesses will need to effectively link information technology and operations much more so than in the past to accomplish movement to this new baseline. Only certain inputs, such as access to traditional workforces or centralized business infrastructure, are constrained. On the output side, abundance is increasingly produced in such great quantities that it would overshadow shortcomings in the business side.

- *Sustainable value moving from business transactions to relationships.* This represents the growing realization that the traditional business transaction as the core source of organizational value is diminishing. Value now comes from relationship dynamics, so it's more important to have community capacity to create on demand than it is to have stocks of inventory or knowledge, which quickly age and become irrelevant. The relationships and their ability to produce what is needed in the moment matter more in a fast-moving, real-time marketplace. Among the many implications are using new management methods (for example, from top-down command-and-control to community curator and facilitator), tapping into new reservoirs of innovation, adopting new ways of interacting with customers, or driving better tacit interactions. The tenets of social business will ultimately enable organizations to accumulate deep reservoirs of relationship capital.

- *Industries in flux with new ones emerging.* Previously stable industries, such as finance and media, are feeling the pinch the strongest, but most others will be disrupted as well. The Great Recession has created a bigger gap between healthy and unhealthy businesses, while many industries are being unbundled or transformed into new ones (for example, software as a service and cloud computing, or the rise of crowdsourcing competing with outsourcing at the low end). Today's dynamic Web-driven global knowledge flows and agile online models for computing and collaboration—as well as economic and intellectual production—are now a leading change agent.

- *Moving from change as the exception to change as the norm.* The world is already seeing faster consumer behavior shifts, quicker pricing changes, more rapid product cycles, and faster media feedback loops. This can lead to more extreme market conditions, but it also opens opportunities to be turned into bottom-line impact for organizations that can adapt to market realities quickly enough. The network is the culprit (and solution) for much of this. We now have pervasive social media instantly transmitting and shaping cultural phenomena and faster financial cause-and-effect in the markets, real-time online markets, and so on. Following a plan is increasingly less important than responding actively and effectively to change.

- *A shift of control to the edge of organizations.* This has been accurately predicted at least as far back as the Cluetrain Manifesto, which said that because of a direct result of the user-shaped Internet, "markets are getting smarter—and getting smarter faster than companies."[5] It's not even really a shift; it's more of an addition of a new dimension to how business operates organizationally and is the hallmark of social business. This new addition changes the dynamics of where useful information comes from, how decisions are made in an organization, and how more autonomy and self-determination will be needed—and tolerated—in modern organizations to meet more dynamic and changing global workplaces comprised of communities instead of traditional employees.

Putting together all of the concepts that have been presented here so far into a strategic plan to redesign an organization can seem like a daunting task. Multiple forces are competing for change today. A vast legacy landscape of existing business models, customer needs, learned behaviors, and instilled culture must be overcome. Fortunately, a large part of the early transition to social business is not only incremental but naturally complements what most organizations are already doing today with their early forays into social media. Whether it's social marketing, social customer relationship management, social collaboration, or social product development, getting started is not the big challenge. The real challenge is acting strategically enough to matter.

Part One has presented a number of successful social business case studies that have illuminated key strategies, as well as the proposition that organizations will have to change in order to transform how they engage the marketplace, produce output, generate revenue, and even define their very existence. In Part Two, we take a much more detailed look at the specific techniques of social business, how they are effectively used, and how to be successful at applying them in a large organization as part of a strategic change management process.

THE TECHNIQUES OF SOCIAL BUSINESS

Chapter 6

Social Media Marketing

Marketing departments were among the earliest adopters within most businesses to start applying social media. It wasn't long after blogs and social networks arrived on the scene in a major way in the mid-2000s that marketers began using these emerging online tools. Although they often used social media very much like the traditional push channels that came before them—such as print, radio, and television—they also grappled with and learned to work through the unique challenges and opportunities of the new two-way communications environment that social media appeared to offer.

The early days of social media marketing proved instructional for brands. The lessons from pioneers came fast and furious for those who watched closely. Major companies started blogs, with some even giving a blog to any to employee who wanted one. A great deal of experimentation with sites that were new at the time like MySpace and emerging tactics like influencer outreach ensued. Now, most large companies have Twitter accounts and Facebook pages, combined with a smattering of other social media presences.[1] Some early adopters achieved significant wins with online communities, engaging effectively and strategically with their existing customers. The big winners didn't necessarily trumpet their successes, however, and so it was years before the market was clear on what worked and what didn't.

Given the perceived lack of clear-cut, widely broadcast success stories, a commonly held view of social media marketing in the early years was that it showed potential but might not drive meaningful business results. However, as demonstrated in stories like P&G's knock-out hit with the Old Spice campaign, engaging with the world through social media can produce widespread results regardless of target audience. Indeed, studies show that social media marketing can be employed effectively for high-impact bottom-line results in terms of sales revenue and profits. Along with financial benefits come closely related outcomes such as improved products, more efficiency, and a deeper connection to the marketplace, as well as happier, more satisfied customers.

In late 2010, McKinsey & Company surveyed over thirty-two hundred executives from a wide range of industries, regions, and internal functions and explored the impact of social technologies on their business. In terms of marketing, 63 percent of respondents reported that social media improved marketing effectiveness. The median improvement, given the fledgling adoption compared to more traditional approaches, was notable, with solid double-digit gains in awareness, consideration, conversation, and loyalty (see Figure 6.1).

Participation is the key to making social media marketing work. Creating a participatory environment conducive to driving business results relies on two general tenets:

Social Business Tenet #6
Participation can take any direction. Be prepared for it, and take advantage of it.

Social business activities encourage open, widespread collaboration and capture value from the resulting inputs through the processes of curating, moderating, and analyzing the contributions of participants. Social media marketing efforts start by targeting particular audiences and draw in varied participants who can take

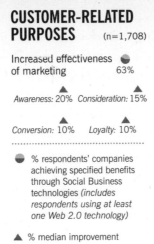

CUSTOMER-RELATED PURPOSES (n=1,708)

Increased effectiveness
of marketing   63%

Awareness: 20%   *Consideration:* 15%

Conversion: 10%   *Loyalty:* 10%

....

% respondents' companies
achieving specified benefits
through Social Business
technologies *(includes
respondents using at least
one Web 2.0 technology)*

▲ % median improvement

Figure 6.1   **Social Media Marketing Benefits from McKinsey & Company's December 2010 Executive Survey**

Source: Bughin, J., and Chui, M. "The Rise of the Networked Enterprise: Web 2.0 Finds Its Payday." *McKinsey Quarterly*, Dec. 2010.

the conversation in constructive and destructive directions. Preparation is essential (a full discussion of how to manage communities is explored in Chapter Twelve), and brands must be ready for all types of contributions; prune only the ones that are truly unacceptable (due to legal, regulatory, or policy reasons), and respond to contributions that warrant engagement. The unexpected is often perceived as the enemy of stability and success, but social business practitioners realize it's also the gateway to opportunity.

In fact, nearly every seemingly negative contribution is value in disguise and can be turned into something useful through further engagement. For example, in 2006 General Motors launched a user-generated advertising campaign to promote its Chevy Tahoe SUV with online thirty-second spots, such as vehicle hero shots, majestic mountain scenery, and ability to overlay text on all graphics. Shortly after launch, GM faced an unanticipated and unintended outcome: environmentalists started creating videos with anti-GM messaging that began receiving mainstream media attention. Rather than censor the four hundred videos containing messages like "Don't Buy Me" and "My MPG [miles per gallon] Sucks," GM used the opportunity to highlight positive environmental aspects of the Tahoe, including its best-in-class fuel economy and ability to use renewable fuel, as well as having the highest safety ratings in its segment.

Managing social business efforts, governing results, and dealing with risk are key aspects of applying this social business tenet successfully. This applies particularly to social media marketing, which requires exposing a company's public brand in a seemingly permanent way. The least expected contributions can often have the largest business impact: extracting value from unexpected outcomes requires adept management in the moment, when situations are most unclear and critical difficult to control.

Social Business Tenet #7
Eliminate all potential barriers to participation. Ease of use is essential.

Studies on human interaction have shown that even small increases in the required choices in a process will increase its complexity to a point that it significantly reduces contribution.[2] This is equally true of human interaction in social media. Consider the Chevy Tahoe campaign. To generate a high level of participation, GM had to simplify the extremely complex process of TV commercial production and make intuitive tools available online to novice users. Making user contributions easy was an incredibly difficult process.

Many of the most effective social media services, such as Twitter, which basically consists of a single field to type in status updates, work primarily because of this key tenet.[3] Unfortunately this principle is frequently abandoned in the enterprise, where user interfaces and experiences are overly complicated and overengineered to appear sophisticated or highly capable, while the consumer Internet industry learned long ago that complexity reduces participation and leads to failure.

STRATEGIC APPROACHES TO SOCIAL MEDIA MARKETING

One of the more nuanced aspects of social media marketing is what is known as designing for impact. While many of the requisite superficial activities of social media marketing are necessary and important, such as maintaining company pages and user profiles in social networks, these activities in isolation won't do much to align the marketing process with the organization's social business vision. Traditional marketing has its own life cycle intent on identifying customers, satisfying them, and retaining them as long as possible. Marketing has become a sophisticated discipline that encompasses demographics, social sciences, psychology, anthropology, and other fields to maximize the effect of messages transmitted to the marketplace, so as to help customers find the company and generate demand for its products and services.

In social media marketing, the objectives of customer acquisition, satisfaction, and retention remain, but relationship management requires fundamental rethinking. Whereas it was reasonably straightforward to understand the marketing numbers game (reach, response rate, conversation ratio, and so on) in a limited number of large channels using well-defined and branded marketing messages, social media marketing is different. A substantially greater number of channels with less structure are available for social media marketing: hundreds of social networks, special interest online communities, blogs, and other unique forms of social media that may contain relevant audiences. Identifying and segmenting audiences can be challenging and highly inefficient.

But identifying the suitable social media segments to engage with is only half of the challenge of maximizing the impact of social media marketing. The other challenge is figuring out the best type (or combination of types) of social media to use. There are four major strategic approaches to marketing with social media (see Figure 6.2):

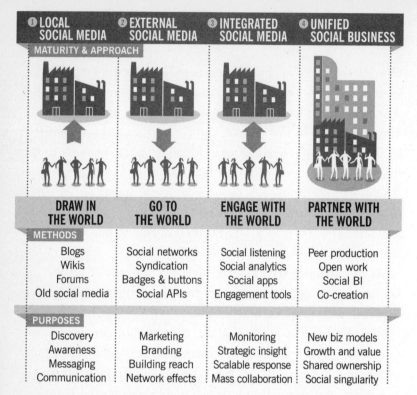

Figure 6.2   **Methods of Engagement in Social Media Marketing**

Note: API = application programming interface; BI = business intelligence

- *Local social media.* This was primarily the choice in the early days, with companies creating their own blogs, discussion forums, and online communities on sites they created and controlled. This approach allows companies to retain a high level of control over experiences and content. For example, the Nuts About Southwest blog serves as a media outlet for Southwest Airlines to supplement traditional corporate communications around brand messaging and crisis management.
- *External social media.* Social media started out as a highly fragmented space, consisting of millions of individual publishing outlets and only a few large, central social media sites such as MySpace and

YouTube (and even these were limited to a few million people at first). Over time, global social networks started aggregating audiences of meaningful size, attracting a critical mass of users and brands. Brands can use both mass and niche social media outlets for maximum impact. For example, Levi's launched a promotion on World Water Day in 2011 to support a new product launch of jeans using a reduced-water manufacturing process. The brand partnered with Water.org to create a game experience that would educate participants on global water issues. Participation by the community would unlock Levi's contribution of up to 200 million liters of clean drinking water at predetermined levels of contribution. Users were encouraged to complete activities on different platforms, including a pledge on Facebook, a check-in on Foursquare, sending a message on Twitter, and answering a question on Yahoo! The campaign drove foot traffic to Levi's retail stores (and subsequent sales), and the user community triggered the full charitable donation to sustainable water programs around the world.

• *Integrated social media.* Multichannel efforts target multiple aspects of user brand engagement, combining local and external social media as well as offline experiences. Integrated approaches combine a variety of social venues into a consistent, up-to-date, and synchronized social media experience, priming large audiences for deeper subsequent engagement. An example of a major integrated experience driving significant results was *True Blood*'s Facebook application used to promote the third season of the HBO hit show (see Figure 6.3). HBO's marketing firm hired Stuzo | Dachis Group to build a multilevel interactive social media party experience embedded in Facebook where fans could select their favorite character from the show and submit their city information to win passes to an exclusive local screening event. The real-time geographical results were displayed on a custom heat map. To encourage sustained engagement and reinforce the June 13 screening event date, passes were awarded every six minutes and thirteen seconds. In addition, fans could win True Blood gear, send virtual gear to Facebook friends, and be eligible for a grand

Figure 6.3   HBO's *True Blood* Facebook Marketing Application: An
Integrated Social Experience

prize. The promotion drove an additional 750,000 visitors to HBO's True Blood page, helped increase the number of Facebook "Likes" by 115 percent to 3 million, and contributed to nearly doubling the number of third season premiere viewers to 6.4 million.

- *Unified social businesses.* At the far end of the spectrum lies what appears to be ahead: businesses where the boundaries between workers, customers, and partners are blurred. In terms of marketing, those who are engaged the most deeply may indeed be employees—or they may just as easily be customers, potential customers, or workers from a trading partner. For example, community-powered apparel firm Threadless is a popular T-shirt production service that began in 2000 with the premise that anybody (customers or otherwise) could design its shirts. A thriving community of independent designers contributes over fifteen designs in an average week; designs are then rated by customers on a scale to help determine which designs will be produced. Threadless has expanded beyond T-shirts to other product lines designed in the same way. But as in a typical social business, Threadless's product designers are not employed by the company and a large portion of design influence comes from customers.[4] User participation greatly reduces the cost to design, market, sell, and produce products. In the Threadless social business model, anyone can contribute designs or opinions, and everyone benefits from the result.

Activating these four strategic approaches requires effective execution of tactics. As the old saying goes, the devil is in the details.

GETTING TO RETURN ON INVESTMENT WITH SOCIAL MEDIA MARKETING

Chief marketing officers and business managers need to know what returns they can expect by engaging in social business methods for marketing. Measuring value and calculating return on investment can be accomplished with a combination of existing and emerging techniques. Calculating return on investment can be difficult unless all factors are known. But most businesses should have a set of key performance indicators (KPIs) already in place that are linked to value creation and currently being collected. Linking social media marketing programs to existing KPIs is the most direct method for determining if efforts benefit the organization and deliver results cost-effectively. Common KPIs used to measure and compare the results of social media marketing are number of leads generated, leads to opportunity conversions, value of sales against campaign spending, and an increase in brand awareness scores.

Emerging techniques for measuring return on investment can be derived from the mechanics of social business activity by participants. These KPIs are much more experimental but good for conveying the approaches that new methods of operation and interaction create. Useful social media marketing KPIs include:

- Percentage of effective marketing content derived externally
- Percentage of leads generated by customer advocacy
- Value of sales closed primarily because of customer advocacy

Good social media marketing shares and decentralizes efforts in reaching, involving, engaging, contributing, supporting, and doing business with customers across lines of business. Successful marketing departments will find themselves positioned as architects of collaborative processes leading to desired business outcomes. Looked at through this lens, return on investment never looked so good, though the process of getting to the top of the maturity curve will take years and survival of more than a few social media crises.

THE VIRTUOUS SOCIAL BUSINESS CYCLE: LISTENING AND ENGAGEMENT

Most organizations that start to engage in social media marketing— or any other kind of social business activity for that matter—soon run into a challenge. Once they begin opening up to a wider audience, the sheer size of resulting participation quickly overwhelms a company's capacity to listen, much less respond, to what the world is saying. This isn't an issue for traditional marketing approaches: one-way communication may reach millions of listeners, but brands are not expected to engage in a sustained conversation. By contrast, in social media marketing, consumers, prospects, shareholders, activists, and other participants expect dialogue. Nonresponse can lead to damaged brand and reputation; however, most companies underestimate the level of effort required when getting started.

The emerging field of social media analytics has enabled brands to listen at scale and gain insight into the general public's perception of a company's actions and statements. By examining social media data for different time periods, businesses can understand how public relations policies and marketing efforts have changed general opinion. Consider the situation of global auto manufacturer Toyota in late 2009, when a spate of high-profile vehicle recalls started to have an impact on multiple brands in the global automotive industry. Toyota faced a recall over faulty accelerators and had to navigate a communications crisis amplified by social media.

Toyota wasn't the only manufacturer experiencing a recall, but a growing chorus of media, consumer, and governmental voices seemed to focus on Toyota. At the time, to get a sense of how large-scale discussions in social media were affecting the perception of the industry, Internet monitoring firm Webtrends examined the social media discussions involving well-known automotive brands undergoing recalls, including BMW, Audi, Peugeot, Citroen, and Honda.[5] During the peak of the global furor around these recalls, Webtrends used social analytics to create a picture of marketplace sentiment and determine which brands were dealing well with the impact of the media firestorm taking place.

Damien Hews, a social measurement specialist for Webtrends, analyzed the leading topics of conversation involving the automotive industry in various social media across the Internet. As expected, Toyota was at the top of the public's mind. Of the six brands analyzed, Toyota far and away dominated social media discussions.

Over 400,000 posts out of nearly 1 million relating to the six brands mentioned Toyota during the two weeks in 2010 that Webtrends analyzed the social data. Said Hews of the data at the time: "Delving deeper into the analysis, I wanted to learn more about the tone of people's conversations regarding the brands. Toyota was mentioned over 11,000 times; of which 64% of the dialogue was negative." In comparison, social media discussions relating to other brands made evident Toyota's inability to respond effectively. Hews observed that Honda's "key words mentioned in 5,866 posts have been predominantly positive." The social media analysis concerning Honda contained a decidedly different result, with mentions of "quality," "hero," and "airbag" appearing next to the word "recall." This strongly suggested that although Honda also had to recall over 1 million vehicles because of airbag issues, its communication management efforts had been more effective than Toyota's.

What was fascinating about this event, which played out in the media dramatically for several months and involved many of automotive's largest brands, was that Peugeot and Citroen remained almost completely untouched by their recall issues in the social media arena. BMW had the strongest showing of sentiment in the social media channels analyzed, with approximately 200,000 mentions of the brand over the same time period and almost none mentioning its recall. Hews reported that "discussions relating to the brand have included words such as 'stunts', 'performance' and other premium brand names such as 'Mercedes' and 'Audi' both being mentioned in discussions relating to the BMW brand."[6]

Ultimately Toyota was roundly criticized for mishandling its social media strategy. Hundreds of millions of its customers were using social networks, and the company did little to engage and address the negative messages that were repeated and amplified, undermining efforts when the brand finally began to respond in a limited fashion through services such as Digg.[7] In the fast-moving world of social media, a company's lack of social presence means that it completely loses the ability to influence the message or connect with and shape the perception of the public in any way. Brands must invest the time to monitor what the collective consciousness of social media is thinking about the company, its product and services, and be ready to engage and respond.

Toyota's efforts started only after considerable damage was done.[8] YouGov's brand index, which is based on a poll of five thousand people per day, positioned Toyota at the top of the index at the beginning of 2010, but it soon plummeted far below the other major auto manufacturers (see Figure 6.4). It wasn't until the February 8 appearance on DiggDialogue by Jim Lenz, president of Toyota's North American sales operations, that the numbers began to turn around. The appearance garnered over thirty-two hundred comments, an engagement level that typically only celebrities achieve, showing the intense public interest in the subject. But the damage was permanently inflicted on Toyota's closely guarded reputation.

It's clear in retrospect that the incalculable financial and competitive impact, given Toyota's sterling global reputation prior to the recall, could have been mitigated with better communications. It's a story, however, that is commonplace given the sudden appearance

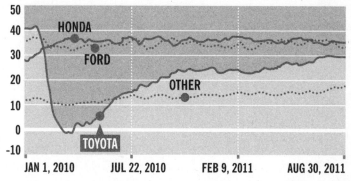

Figure 6.4 Toyota's Slide in Public Perception, January 2010– August 2011

Source: YouGov.com.

of social media on the global stage: unprepared companies continue to experience the disruptive effects of new global knowledge flows in social media that they'd previously disregarded. By the time Lenz made his appearance in social media, it was far too late. Listening and responding need to be real-time in social media. Effective social marketing is built on a strong foundation of continuous listening and effective engagement.

Another major brand affected by emergent bottom-up influence the same year as Toyota was oil multinational juggernaut British Petroleum (BP). Following the catastrophic accident on the Deepwater Horizon oil drilling rig in 2010, oil flowed unabated into the Gulf of Mexico for three months, resulting in the largest oil spill in U.S. history. The BP crisis communications team, instead of being an effective voice for the company in managing the unfolding situation, quickly became the target of social media. BP's social media participation, despite millions of urgent global conversations taking place concerning the company, was largely limited to formal pronouncements in traditional channels that were largely repeated or referenced from the company's official Twitter account. Soon after the oil rig disaster struck, an individual with the pseudonym Leroy Stick launched a Twitter account known as @BPGlobalPR, which he used to satirize the starched and formal tone of PR messages from the BP crisis communications team. What began as Stick's personal outlet for expressing frustration through humor and parody quickly grew into one of the more effective and widely repeated commentaries on the crisis.[9]

BP's own social media was not nearly as effective as Leroy Stick's, and even three years after the crisis, the unofficial and incendiary @BPGlobalPR Twitter account still had five times as many followers as BP's official account.[10] Many sources credited @BPGlobalPR as being more interesting, relevant, and informative than anything BP provided during the crisis, while also portraying the oil giant's attempts to deal with the situation as inept and bumbling.

Like Toyota, BP's reputation rapidly sank to even further depths than the car manufacturer experienced, and it stayed there.

The formal, controlled language and tone of traditional business communication (press releases, news wires, press conferences, TV and radio spots, corporate communication areas on company sites) is not the language used in effective social media engagement. BP's story is just one of many suggesting that social media engagement must be more personal and direct in nature. Language needs to be conversational and casual, as in personal face-to-face communication. Humor and self-deprecation, as in real life, are also highly valued but must be used with care and in the cultural and regional context. Scaling engagement can be challenging, but people expect personalized conversations.

These stories and the many others like them therefore lead to two more tenets of social business, both crucial to success in social media marketing, but also in virtually any social business activity or process:

Social Business Tenet #8
Listen to and engage continuously with all relevant social business conversations.

This approach of listening and engaging continuously has been debated and criticized as unsustainable. Before the rise of social media monitoring and analytics, a case could have been made that this approach was impossible for most organizations. Listening across the entirety of social media and then successfully identifying important conversations would require too large a staff or too much time. But in the era of sophisticated tools that enable monitoring of a surprisingly large portion of the many corners and edges of social media, it's now entirely possible for largely automated methods to provide the thorough coverage of social media on a near real-time basis. Most organizations can avoid becoming a Toyota or BP and instead effectively listen to and engage in social business conversations.

Social Business Tenet #9
The tone and language of social business are most effective when they're casual and human.

The language of everyday conversation is the language of social business. Although some cultures are more formal than others (Japan is a well-known example of business formality), social media provide an effective way to connect people when technology helps mediate among parties who often don't know each other very well. Companies must listen to all potential stakeholders and engage in meaningful conversations with simple, natural, and personal phrases that are understandable and clear.

A high-profile social media crisis driven by external forces, as with Toyota and BP, can be a worst-case situation for large companies, which are often unprepared and take too long in today's rapid information cycles to organize and respond. However, for others, these cases are the most critical examples of how companies can turn a tide of negative sentiment into a benefit and transform situations into major opportunities to build reputation and brand.

In late 2008, Ford Motor Company targeted the operator of a small Ford Ranger online fan site called TheRangerStation.com for infringing on its trademark and intellectual property rights. Ford issued a cease-and-desist letter to the Web site's owner, Jim Oaks, and demanded payment of five thousand dollars in fines, in addition to turning the domain name over to Ford. At the time, Oak had run the site for ten years and lacked the resources to fight the automotive company in the courts.[11] Consequently, he reached out to the only significant resource he had, the site's members as well as the world at large, by posting the story of Ford's action out in the open in his blog. Within twenty-four hours, there were nearly a thousand indignant responses, many of them openly hostile to Ford and disappointed that Ford was treating its loyal customers, as well as passionate brand advocates, in this way.

For its part, Ford followed a standard process to stop sites from selling counterfeit products by threatening legal action, which was usually enough to get them to close up shop. But although Jim's site was technically in violation of Ford's legal rights, it was also unlike most other sites that Ford encountered because TheRanger Station.com fostered a community of Ford loyalists. Ford also had a manager who could listen and engage in a personal, direct manner.

Scott Monty, Ford's global digital and multimedia communications manager, became aware of the "Ranger Station" situation by a tweet within hours after Jim's post. Instead of waiting days or weeks to go through a formal response process involving discussions with the legal, brand, and compliance folks at Ford, Monty quickly responded over Twitter, saying he'd investigate the issue. Over the course of a single day, Monty kept the public updated on his conversations with Ford internal departments and answered user questions as the story gained greater publicity. By the end of the workday, Ford and Jim Oaks had reached an agreement. Monty's rapid action had quickly defused the situation before it became fodder for traditional media and a potentially much larger social media crisis.

Ford was fortunate that Monty was able to listen and engage rather than hide behind formal policies or legal statutes. He simply talked to those watching the situation in everyday language and explained what he was doing. By avoiding legalese and being open, helpful, and informative—in other words, engaging in conversation—he avoided a potentially far worse outcome and aided directly in the successful resolution of the problem. Even more important, he changed the perception of Ford's actions at the end, turning what looked like a heavy-handed legal move that harmed a seemingly innocent person into a story of unfortunate but necessary behavior by the company. The final message was one of a positive outcome that benefited both Ford and Jim Oaks.[12]

Most social media marketing does not consist of identifying and turning crisis situations. However, all organizations must be ready to listen and engage. These capabilities are fundamental to social business success. As organizations evolve, listening, engagement, and analysis have rapidly matured into a sophisticated discipline known as social business intelligence.

SOCIAL BUSINESS INTELLIGENCE: NEXT-GENERATION LISTENING AND ENGAGEMENT

Social business intelligence helps companies extend listening and engagement by applying insights across business processes and targeted business outcomes beyond marketing communications (Figure 6.5). Specific responses to social business intelligence insights depend on the nature of the analysis. For example, outcomes can be strategic and affect how a company evolves its products and services. They can also be tactical, on-the-ground insights that drive individual interaction or collaboration with prospects, customers, business partners, and others.

The number of examples of social business intelligence driving key business outcomes is rapidly growing.

Marketing Optimization

Marketers were early adopters of corporate social media, and they have also been some of the first to explore applications of social business intelligence. In addition to reports and dashboards that provide raw data such as visitor counts and number of retweets, marketers are able to determine why events occurred. With social business intelligence, companies can craft detailed yet fully integrated qualitative pictures of the inbound funnel, identify why engagement strategies are working or not, and organize systematic yet mass-customized responses in scale. A prime example is U.S. Cellular's ability to measure the successful impact of a social business activity by using the Dachis Group's Social Business Index (SBI), a big data analytics service that measures the effectiveness of corporate social

Figure 6.5   Taking Social Listening and Engagement to a New Level:
Social Business Intelligence

engagement with its ecosystem of customers, partners, and influencers. The index ranks companies with respect to each other: a lower number means a higher overall effective level of social business performance.

Launching a new social marketing campaign in September 2011, U.S. Cellular wanted to track its effectiveness to see if it was engaging potential customers better than in the past. By monitoring its ranking in the SBI (which steadily rose from 600 at the outset to 120 by late 2010), the company could see how its actions affected performance. By using social business intelligence, it understood far more about the actual campaign results than just raw traffic numbers. Visitor statistics alone can reflect positive outcomes (enjoying the message) or negative results (from critical or mocking references in social media) depending on the situation, inflating results. Natural language processing and pattern matching was used to gauge intent and sentiment to determine if the U.S. Cellular marketing campaign was creating desired outcomes and levels of engagement.

Capturing Ideas and Unmet Needs

Going beyond trend analysis of analytics allows processing and isolation of deeper implications of social media activity. Social business intelligence can identify innovation opportunities, new ideas from the marketplace, customer wants and desires, and the gaps in an organization's services.

Situational Awareness

Social business intelligence enables companies to identify and track top trends, understand when critical situations arise to protect customer experience and brand reputation, and more. Going beyond low-level analytics, social business intelligence can help make sense of big data more deeply than other manual analytical processes can.

Customer Care Opportunities

By fully empowering social customer relationship management, social business intelligence augments interactions with customers in social media by improving triage, prioritization, and resolution processes within customer care. Telecommunications provider Comcast brought the possibility of using Twitter for customer service to the world's attention with one manager's use of the platform to engage customers. Today companies including Dell and Time Warner use social analytics and social business intelligence processes to identify customer care situations and address them as needed.[13]

Sentiment Analysis

While social analytics provides basic insight into a customer's state of mind, more sophisticated methods of social business intelligence can semantically process and assess the actual meaning of the social media conversations involving a company or its products in order to derive actionable insight and market research.

In the following chapters, we explore how social business intelligence can be applied in specific business applications.

Chapter 7

Social Product Development

W ho can help a company design its next product better than its own customers? Traditional approaches to product development involve customers to some extent, while social business approaches transform the legacy process to achieve better outcomes. Most large companies maintain long-standing product development processes, often involving proprietary formulations, patents, and other intellectual property and critical methods. However, recent studies show that up to 80 percent of all new product introductions ultimately fail, leaving a lot of room for improvement given that a product failure can sink an entire chain of investment from R&D, marketing, sales, distribution, partnership overhead, manufacturing, and so on.[1] Social product development can lead to products that more closely meet customer needs, resulting in more successful products that are more resilient to disruption and changes in the marketplace.

Wireless technology company Precyse had an engineering resource problem: it needed to develop an improved radio frequency identification (RFID) monitoring product but had limits on its internal capabilities. It reached out to InnoCentive, a crowdsourcing company in Waltham, Massachusetts, that maintains communities of experts. InnoCentive design facilitators helped Precyse create a design challenge that eventually produced the Smart Agent Device and saved the company $250,000. Rom Eizenberg, Precyse's chief marketing officer, observed "[The community] delivered not just a solution, but also the algorithm and calculations that proved the solution could be done."[2]

The concept of shared creation, like the one accomplished by Precyse, appears in many social business stories presented in this book, such as Threadless T-shirt designs, the FoldIt AIDS virus solution explored in Chapter Four, and Intuit's customers helping create customer service. Opening up the creative process beyond organizational boundaries achieves a far richer set of inputs. Once these are evaluated, this richness can flow through the entire product development process, providing many more options, innovations, and new ways of recasting both problem statements and solutions.

Every business is vastly outnumbered by customers and potential customers. Placing a bureaucratic, centralized product development team into the critical path of open, ongoing product design is no longer an efficient or productive application of the resources at hand needed to solve customer problems. With virtually everyone in the developed world online, the biggest sources of talent, engagement, innovation, agility, and workers reside on the network, which increasingly means social channels. Product developers can now engage with the network at scale using mass collaboration techniques and technologies to tweak, tune, refine, contribute, and even completely reinvent a company's products and services. Increasingly innovation exchange platforms are emerging that cultivate communities of design talent around topics of interest that companies can easily plug into their social product development process. Subjects range widely, including graphic design (Crowdspring), grant writing (Philoptima), scientific and engineering problems (InnoCentive), software development (TopCoder), and many other disciplines.

Social product development often starts as a surprisingly simple activity and grows steadily more sophisticated over time (see Figure 7.1).

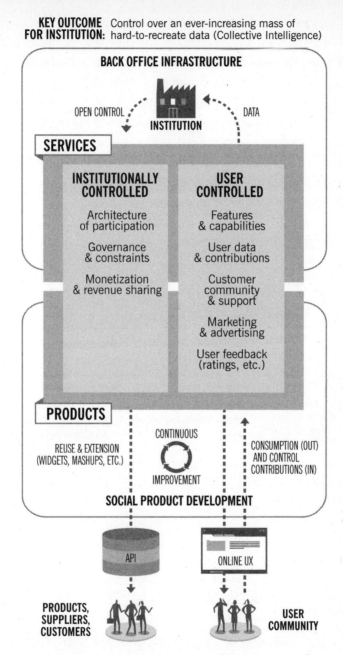

Figure 7.1 The Social Product Development Process

The process usually begins with a collection of implicit user contributions, leveraging something Internet luminary John Battelle called the Database of Intentions.[3] Companies automate real-time feedback loops to identify customer behaviors, desires, frequent activities, and other information that can be played back for future users. In later iterations, social product development cycles elicit explicit contributions on desired colors, features, and other useful attributes. For example, LG supports a yearly open community effort for designing next-generation telephones, in which designers from around the world compete against each other in a community-based environment.[4]

One of the best ways to understand the full scope of social product development is to compare it with traditional product development, shown in Figure 7.2.

	Traditional Product Development	Social Product Development
Customer interaction method	Telephone, mail, face-to-face, one-way media (print, TV, radio), e-mail	Internet, e-mail, social media, custom-designed social experiences, innovation exchange platforms
Largest source of innovation	Organizations	Customers and the marketplace
Innovation cycle time	Months, years	Minutes, hours, days
Feedback mechanisms	Market research, surveys, complaints, suggestions, focus groups	Analytics, social media interactions, explicit external contributions
Customer engagement style	Controlled, well-defined process	Spontaneous and chaotic

Figure 7.2   Reconceiving Product Development with Social Business

	Traditional Product Development	Social Product Development
Product development process	Centralized, up-front design	Some up front, remainder is emergent and decentralized
Product architecture	Closed, not designed for easy extension or reuse by others; walled garden	Open and easy to refine, change, and extend; design (and legal) for widespread remixing and reintegration
Product development culture	Hierarchical, centralized, private, closed, somewhat collaborative, expert driven	Egalitarian, diverse, highly open and collaborative, collective intelligence
Product testing	Internal, dedicated test groups, hand-picked select customers	World as testers
Customer support	Customer service	Customer community
Product promotion	One-way marketing and advertising	Viral propagation, social marketing, network effects, word-of-mouth
Business model	Product sales, customer service and support fees, access charges	Advertising, subscriptions, product sales, mass customization, unintended uses (by others)
Customer relationship	External buyer (consumer)	Partners and suppliers (consumer as producers)
Product ownership	Institution, executive management and shareholders	Entire ecosystem (business, communities of customers and partners)
Partnering process	Formal, explicit, infrequent, mediated	Ad hoc, real time, thousands of online partners, disintermediated
Product Development and Integration Tools	Heavyweight, formal, complex, expensive, time-consuming, enterprise oriented	Lightweight, informal, simple, free, fast, consumer oriented

Figure 7.2   *(continued)*

	Traditional Product Development	Social Product Development
Competitive advantage	Superior products, legal barriers to entry (intellectual property protections), brand name advantage, price, popularity, distribution channel control	Network effect, effective community throughput, mass customization, control over difficult-to-recreate information, end user ownership, ease of use, cost-effectiveness, audience size, best-of-breed participation

Figure 7.2   *(continued)*

Most improvement from social product development will be achieved incrementally. The risks are often lower since company brands and reputations are much less at stake for most of the development process. However, the major shifts required to reach the most effective aspects of the approach, such as new business models, encouraging unintended uses, and mass customization, require more deliberate transformation of company strategy and organization. The specific techniques and change management processes required will be explored in Part Three, which turns to the details of how to achieve the deeper changes required to more fully reach the potential of social product development.

Chapter 8

Crowdsourcing

Community-Powered Workforces

The notion of the Internet as the leading medium for self-expression and creativity certainly is no longer novel. Social media have shown that online services can tap into a wellspring of global innovation and change industry dynamics. As social business begins to show how innovative work can blur boundaries between organizations and customers on one side and business partners on the other, traditional businesses have found ways to use this shift to their advantage.

It's not an accident that some of the largest and most widely used online sites are Google, Facebook, YouTube, and Wikipedia.[1] The vast majority of all content on the last three services is entirely user generated, while the first, Google, is merely a reflection of the world's own information after passing through a highly secret patented algorithm. Collectively created content has become the most significant and popular part of the Web.

A BRIEF PRIMER ON CROWDSOURCING

A new, slightly different take on user-generated content has emerged through what is known as crowdsourcing. Due to its increased popularity in both social and business circles, a growing range of online products and services specializes in meeting specific business needs by enlisting niche communities to tackle challenges, often in exchange for some form of compensation. At first, crowdsourcing might seem closely related to social product development, but whereas social product development focuses on a specific yet important step in a company's R&D effort, crowdsourcing focuses on less intellectual work and consists of literally any form of participation required to accomplish a business objective. The advantages are clear: extremely low-cost access to enthusiasts and experts on a given subject matter or task, broader input of new ideas, faster design of business solutions, and a quicker response to business needs. The disadvantages can often be less clear, but they do exist. These usually break down to the perceived lack of control, randomness of the process, quality of the outcome, ownership of intellectual property and the eventual result, and worries about security and privacy.

One of the earliest, most effective examples of corporate crowdsourcing occurred in 2006 when the company now known as SiriusXM decided, after many attempts at trying to make its less popular stations more appealing, that its customers might do better at programming its radio stations. It opened the playlist of one of its least popular radio stations to user voting online and by phone. Almost immediately, the resulting channel was a runaway hit, and despite periodic changes over the years to adjust the way customers participate, it remains the company's most popular station (and single content product).[2]

But can sourcing meaningful work to the social world be a repeatable, reliable way to run a business? Can organizations rely on largely unknown groups of contributors to predictably provide outputs to support day-to-day operations? While the fast-growing number of successful crowdsourcing examples in companies large and small speaks volumes, an important confirmation and new data point surfaced in 2010 that shows that the wellspring might indeed be as large as required for widespread application of crowdsourcing.[3]

61% WILLING

Figure 8.1 Percentage of Customers Willing to Cocreate

A broad survey of consumers from Forrester Research showed that despite half of all companies at the time having yet to use social media to drive product design, creation, or strategy, approximately "sixty-one percent of all US online adults are willing co-creators" if they are so tapped (Figure 8.1).[4]

Crowdsourcing options exist to service the divergent needs of businesses small to large. For example, increasingly capable and mature enterprise crowdsourcing services such as Microtask are available to large companies with scale and security concerns. Microtask is an enterprise work platform that processes billions of crowdsourced tasks per year for businesses. In order to protect the intellectual property of its customers, businesses concerned with sending sensitive data outside the company can operate Microtask's software themselves yet still take advantage of remote distributed output. Other crowdsourcing services, such as Tongal and Whinot, support individuals and small businesses as the majority of their customer base. Crowdsourcing offers a less expensive option for conducting activities that small business may not be able to otherwise afford, such as tapping into expert advice or creative production resources (Figure 8.2).

MOVING TO CROWDSOURCING: A PROCESS

For organizations ready to shift more productive work to the network, there is an increasingly well-defined set of best practices emerging on how to apply crowdsourcing to their lines of business with the least

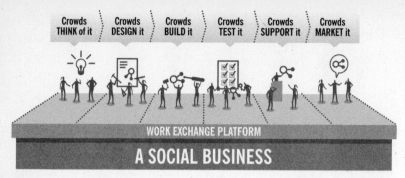

| Crowds THINK of it | Crowds DESIGN it | Crowds BUILD it | Crowds TEST it | Crowds SUPPORT it | Crowds MARKET it |

WORK EXCHANGE PLATFORM

A SOCIAL BUSINESS

Figure 8.2 Using Crowdsourcing for the Full Range of Business Activities

disruption and most direct benefit. Businesses looking to explore this new approach to sourcing work can follow these commonsense steps:

- *Identify areas where traditional methods aren't working in the business today.* This might be in customer support, where the crowdsourcing aspect of customer relationship management can offer significant help, or it could be in product design, testing, or other areas where not enough people with the right ideas or skills currently reside within the organization. When a business function is far too expensive, doesn't scale, or is producing poor-quality results, often because of a scarcity of usable inputs, it's a good candidate for being crowdsourced.

- *Create a short list of candidate crowdsourcing services.* It can help to identify more than one service in order to test options in parallel to get the best results. Maturity levels and capacity of services vary widely based on the core function they provide. New services are emerging regularly, however, so it's usually worth taking time to explore and find the most suitable candidates that align well with the business.

- *Engage in pilots with the top crowdsourcing candidates.* One of the benefits of crowdsourcing is its inexpensive cost versus alternatives like subcontractors or outsourcing. Consequently experimenters can almost always afford to try out many different services until they find one that fits best, often selecting a primary and a backup for business continuity. It's useful to determine which services have different levels of capability (more predictable services are often more expensive than the others) and which communities may have a focus aligned with your primary business.

- *Move successful pilots into operation while cultivating new contributors.* Crowdsourcing has much different operating and performance characteristics from traditional staffing, which is typically much more stable, controllable, and deterministic. It takes time to understand how long work takes and how to make it happen faster or with higher quality. Be prepared to continue discovering and evaluating new services, or consider accessing existing communities to tap into and participate with.

While the crowdsourcing process is laden with change management implications as well as transformational challenges and opportunities, this new discipline is moving out of narrow areas such as graphics design, advertising creation, and image recognition and increasingly into mainstream business. In the early years of social media, it was unclear if the structure and direction needed to turn external participation into valuable business outcomes could be harnessed into something useful. Today crowdsourcing looks to be not only viable for a wide variety of business activities but also a strategic asset and competitive tool in the arsenal of the modern social business.

For now, this nascent approach to using social media models for work offers early adopters a powerful, scalable, and easy-to-use method for developing innovative, high-growth products and services that require an entirely different investment profile and can tackle problems that weren't possible to address using the conventional methods. In Part Three, we examine some of the specific methods for designing crowdsourcing into business processes.

Chapter 9

Social Customer Relationship Management and Customer Communities

Social Customer Care

As social media become more accepted into the strategic operations of enterprises, a new hybrid of social media and customer relationship management (CRM) has emerged to help organizations engage with a wider range of customers and prospects. In 2010, the concept of social CRM began gaining traction with marketing and sales disciplines, becoming a promising combination of records-based CRM and social media engagement. By eliminating the database-centric notion of CRM and decades of inadequate communication channels, the closer relationships and engagement theorized by social CRM can unleash a number of key benefits for companies, though not without a few challenges as well.

SAP's Community Network, described in Chapter One, was a custom solution to a new problem. Today more companies have encountered the same issue and realized that the same solutions apply. Social CRM systematizes approaches like SAP's into a set of off-the-shelf social business solutions for customer engagement, opening a new front line in many businesses where the old ways of engaging with customers are no longer sufficient or even competitive. In 2011, only 6 percent of organizations had implemented social CRM, although a survey of thirty-three hundred companies in late 2011 determined that 56 percent are planning to do so.[1] Research firm Gartner estimates that social CRM will be a $1 billion industry by the end of 2012, reflecting increasing adoption by companies as a common strategy and replacement for existing CRM approaches.[2] By moving proven methods, use patterns, and features into a usable tool set, social CRM promises to be a predictable, reliable model, guided by the tenets of social business, for applying social media to customer relationships.

Many of the social media tools and communities that companies have deployed already to meet CRM needs are good examples of social CRM, despite the industry's focus on optimized, predesigned tools. Whenever social media let customers have a relationship with a business—in other words, interaction that is publicly visible to other customers whenever possible—social CRM can occur. The old CRM model, a closed, asocial mode of customer interaction, is the antithesis of social CRM and much less likely to lead to rewarding outcomes for the business and its customers.

Social CRM paints a vision of creating a deeper, more engaging community-based relationship with an organization's customers and prospects instead of the traditional approach where customers are relegated to a well-defined, rigid communication management process. Because it is one part online community, one part crowd-sourcing, and one part customer self-service, social CRM can create an emergent, collaborative online partnership with customers that can result in an array of improvements to business performance in the customer relationship process. Beyond being just for the benefit of the business, however, customers in social CRM approaches tend to have more control over the customer care process, have more sustained contact with the organizations they care about because they are more likely to obtain what they need, and use self-service, mutually visible participation, collective history, and social conversations to assist each other as much as—and typically much more than—the classic CRM model ever could or even was intended to.

Like many aspects of social business, however, the crowd often has its own thoughts and feeling about how work gets done. For social CRM, this necessarily entails less deterministic control and outcomes at times, although many solutions now zero in on and optimize for predictable and reliable behavior, even if they reduce innovation. The Intuit example in Chapter Three of encouraging customers to help other customers within Live Community is a prime example of the customer care aspect of social CRM in action. A canonical pattern here is this: a social CRM environment will let a visitor ask a question publicly and let anyone else in the community, customer or employee, answer it.

Social CRM tools can also support processes that generate new ideas from a community. Dell's IdeaStorm allows customers to try to solve the company's problems for user and company benefit. For example, users generate an idea such as preinstalling specific software packages, and the community votes on its merit. At the core of making the process work is the question of who decides what the right "official" answer to a customer problem is or which ideas will be selected and how nonemployee submitters will be compensated. These are questions that organizations need to work through in order to transition their customer relationship management to a social business model. We explore how best to determine motivations and rewards for participants in the social business design in Part Three.

By its very nature, social CRM is asymmetrical when it comes to levels of participation; there are always many more customers than workers. Success here is defined by how effectively the resulting social business solution deals with the number of customers who will interact with a business through these new channels while still governing the relationship to make it consistently responsive and successful from a customer perspective. Participation (for example, generating user support questions) must be balanced with equally effective issue communication and resolution, operating within the requirements of corporate policy and commercial law guiding marketing, corporate communications, customer service, consumer privacy, and so on.

Get Satisfaction is a prime example of a targeted social CRM service designed to address the problem of asymmetry in the company-to-customer relationship. Get Satisfaction helps over sixty thousand organizations deal effectively with "conversational scale" from Fortune 500 enterprises to small start-ups—while having consistent policies and procedures for responses to customer-initiated social engagement.[3] Conversational scale is a significant challenge for companies without the right social business tools, because they are so outnumbered by the size of their communities. Although social CRM ultimately includes all customer relationship touch points, Get Satisfaction focuses on customer service inquiry resolution. When a customer arrives at a Get Satisfaction social CRM community looking for help, he or she will ask a question. Get Satisfaction realizes that a million questions from a million customers are far too many to deal with efficiently. Consequently, it puts similar questions into the same bucket. If someone says, "I'm having problem X with your product," and that question has been asked before in a similar fashion, the customer is asked to combine his or her question with that bucket. Because it's a social environment, everyone's questions can be seen and combined when possible. Instead of talking to customers about a million individual issues, only perhaps a few thousand total conversational buckets exist instead, each of which can have a conversational thread on how to resolve the issues contained in it. In fact, that's exactly what happens after enough collective intelligence is built up in the community: when a question is asked and then put in a bucket with other common questions, a solution—and often even a set of solutions—is usually waiting for the customer.

Given that early social CRM providers have focused on only a specific phase of social CRM, it begs the question of the full range of functions that a social CRM solution should have. As with most other aspects of social media, there is now a wide range of social CRM tools, large and small, simple and sophisticated. Therefore, as an organization grows, it will want the option of expanding the nature of the social relationships it maintains with the marketplace, whether marketing, sales, customer service, product development, or other business function. The best social tools aren't overly structured; social media are dynamic and highly fluid, and it's because of this characteristic that so many different outcomes are possible, so tools must be flexible and open-ended to accommodate a wide range of outcomes.

At a minimum, an effective social CRM solution should have four capabilities:

- *A social venue.* Customers must be able to establish a social identity and perceive other customers and their contributions, as well as be able to distinguish the company's workers from other customers. They should be able to interact with both types of parties in the social CRM environment.
- *Customer participation mechanisms.* Although general-purpose discussion forums are open-ended and can be used for many types of participation, they allow customer contributions to head in any direction, productive or otherwise. A little structure, though not enough to kill valuable emergent outcomes, can go a long way. Social CRM becomes more effective and useful when participation mechanisms help guide inputs with specific requirements and toward productive goals. These might include specific features to enable transactions around social customer support, competitive contests, innovation and prediction markets, or joint product design. Some services, such as Kluster, provide finely tuned controls that can be adjusted to find the right mix of structure and open participation. Newer social CRM tools increasingly have pluggable participation applications that let third parties offer rapidly deployable, industry-specific customer relationship solutions—very similar to Apple's successful App Store but aimed at useful customer relationship scenarios.
- *Shared collective intelligence.* Social media are most successful for businesses when focused participation creates a shared repository

of knowledge from combined user participation. Good social CRM tools direct activities of a social CRM environment into accumulated, discoverable, and reusable forms. The artifacts of these activities are customer solutions, product suggestions, sales opportunities, and so on. Successful social CRM creates relationships that get better the more people use them.

• *Mechanisms to deal with conversational scale.* Many businesses still worry that deploying social tools to interact with online customers en masse will create unexpected costs or overhead as thousands—and, in some cases, millions—of customers try to engage with them. Since most existing social media tools have not been designed explicitly to deal with this, this is an area where social CRM tools shine. Service-level agreements that guarantee that customers will get a response if the community at large doesn't deliver or tools that bucket identical inquiries together, as well as other scaling mechanisms, are essential for social CRM to produce effective results.

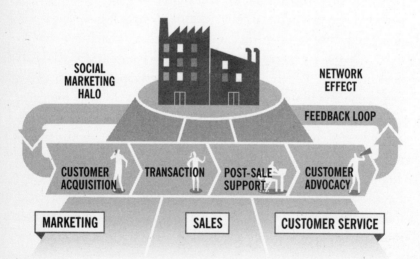

Figure 9.1 The Social CRM Journey

Source: Based on an idea by Jeff Nolan.

Social CRM will be the primary way that traditional organizations will transform customer relationships in the social business era. However, the biggest barrier to adopting social CRM is not the technology, the tools, or customers: rather, it's the mind-set about what CRM can and should accomplish. Social CRM, the recurring lifecycle of which is shown in Figure 9.1, is not about managing customer records or maintaining e-mail blast schedules. It's about forming a close partnership where the organization retains a leadership role and the use of social media results in the creation of vibrant customer community relationships. The elimination of decades of inadequate channels of customer communication will unleash a sudden tide of opportunities, as well as challenges, in the move to social business.

Chapter 10

Social Business Ecosystems

Engaging with Business Partners

S ocial media have never been the exclusive domain of business-to-consumer communications, although mainstream media might create that impression. In fact, companies have been using social media well beyond marketing and customer engagement for quite some time. The value chain formed by the social business continuum includes trading partners, vendors, suppliers, distribution networks, and other business-to-business functions. The example of Teva Pharmaceuticals in Chapter Three shows how social business methods can be expanded to include the supply chain and how companies can improve performance in conjunction with other organizations.

For many companies, the business partner landscape is a competitive environment fraught with shifting relationship dynamics, oversight requirements, and intensive ongoing support and maintenance. It's not uncommon for different departments to interact with the same customer, prospect, or partner, pursuing entirely separate corporate goals. Many partner management strategies reduce relationships to us-versus-them equations that avoid genuine collaboration. This reduces the chance of long-term value growth and innovation. Moreover, having more data about what's happening in the relationship process doesn't guarantee better outcomes. The existing people and processes of partnership management, particularly with affiliate networks and value-added resellers, struggle to filter and stay on top of information overload that comes from the many organizations they must work with and support.

Microsoft's example of supporting its partner network explored at the outset of the book provides an excellent example of business-to-business (B2B) social media used to engage with business partners. However, some readers might take issue with the fact that it's a technology company using technology well and therefore not necessarily indicative of what other industries might be able to achieve. For another example of how relationships with business partners can be transformed with social media, let's look at how some other companies are rethinking the way they operate across their B2B channels.

SOCIAL BUSINESS ECOSYSTEMS: ESSENTIAL EXAMPLES

In 2005, American Express experienced scalability issues as it struggled to support a growing number of small businesses as part of its business expansion. American Express, like Intuit's TurboTax, had discovered that the need for information and support from small organizations was just as intensive—if not more so—as it was for its larger customers. Considering what some companies were already doing with online communities, in 2007 American Express launched the OPEN Forum, an online resource and social networking hub expressly designed for small and medium-sized businesses.

At its core, the idea of OPEN Forum is simple: enable small business owners to communicate and share ideas with each other. As American Express researched the idea initially, it discovered that small business owners were seeking to build better connections with similar business owners, compare ideas and strategy, and network with other businesses where they might be able to find and exchange services. OPEN Forum itself consists of two primary areas. The first element is shared content that's kept in an idea hub. It's a virtual community square where industry experts convey the latest ideas and thought leadership, while small business owners can browse through and comment on the information. American Express found that original, useful, and compelling content was the first step in meeting the large variety of informational needs of its small business customers. By ensuring that content was original and exclusive, American Express established OPEN Forum's reputation as a unique resource that drew participants in increasing numbers after the community was opened up to the public.

The second key element of the OPEN Forum is its social network, which demonstrates social business in action. The social network, available to card members, is called Connectodex: small businesses create a profile, connect or "friend" other business owners, and explain who they are and what their business does. Put simply, Connectodex is a social network designed especially for entrepreneurs. The OPEN Forum provides essential engagement opportunities for customers that American Express can't reasonably provide on its own, especially since it's not a small business itself. Often only another small business can provide the advice or information that another small business owner needs.

The success of OPEN Forum has validated the strength of the initial concept. Only three years after inception, the community was routinely passing the 1 million monthly unique visitors' mark.[1] Thousands of helpful articles are available, and over ten thousand businesses use the service to help each other and use each other's services. American Express derives benefit from the community by employing a smaller customer relationship staff and hosting a valuable service for customers. The forum is also a strong marketing tool because customers use word-of-mouth to recommend the community and its members, as well as the unique and valuable information it contains.[2]

What sets the OPEN Forum example apart is how the service connects customers to each other just as much as it connects them to American Express. By making it easy for customers to help each other in unique and varied ways that no single company could match by itself, American Express's approach cultivates satisfied and successful customers over time without substantially increasing the cost of servicing overhead or dramatically raising the communication level required by the company itself. B2B social business enables cost-effective scaling of partner relations while forging a closer network of relationships among partners that's richer, more diverse, and useful for all parties.

In 2009, the international cosmetics and beauty firm L'Oreal found itself in a situation similar to American Express's as it evaluated its network of salons: over four thousand individual businesses located around the United States. The salons are a key distribution channel for the firm: they are the customers of L'Oreal's high-end cosmetic and beauty supplies in service delivery and a retail sales channel for consumer purchase. As it considered the impact that the sustained recession was having on its business, research confirmed that at least 25 percent of L'Oreal salon customers had been significantly affected by the downturn.[3] This meant that the network of salons used and sold fewer L'Oreal products, which had a ripple effect up the value chain.

As the world's largest cosmetics company, L'Oreal realized that it had the centralized resources to help salons improve the way they engaged with and delivered services to their consumers. Knowing that salons already had the ability to use some Internet tools such as branded Web presence, appointment scheduling, and instructional beauty and makeover videos, L'Oreal decided that it could best help salons by providing them with an avenue to where consumers spent most of their time online: Facebook.

The result was a customer relationship program aimed at making it as easy as possible for salons to create effective interaction with their own consumers within Facebook. L'Oreal used its considerable marketing resources and experience to provide a tool kit for salons to overhaul their Facebook pages. The tool kit included a series of customizable modules that displayed information including salon logo, hours of business, and services provided, as well as a variety of informative and inspirational videos. L'Oreal also provided education for salons on how to use Facebook to engage consumers better. Another long-standing problem for salons was considered as well: appointment scheduling. Useful third-party social applications were incorporated into the tool kit so that salons could offer appointment scheduling through Facebook, making it possible for consumers to initiate new and repeat business with the salons more easily.

Many L'Oreal salons rapidly adopted the social media services, and the efforts were highly effective at incorporating social media into salons to drive business.[4] Stylists were able to forge better direct connections with their clients, and owners benefited from using the more contemporary tools available. The L'Oreal Facebook program went on to win Forrester's 2011 Groundswell award for B2B social media.[5] This example shows how a large business can use social media to connect with business partners better by giving them what they need to improve their own business operations. The solution in this case was self-service social media tools that were business specific (related to the beauty and cosmetics industry) and indirectly applied the tenets of social media such that salons could better build and support their customers.

Engaging with businesses though social media to better support them and help them engage with each other for useful outcomes illustrates the relationship management and support aspect of social business partner life cycle. Another key aspect is creating operating connections with partners through social media as part of a company's supply chain. Known as social supply chain management, this approach is a relative newcomer to social business applications, yet interesting results have started emerging. The Teva Pharmaceuticals example describes the story of an internal supply chain improved with the introduction of social tools. Taking things a step further, another Fortune 500 company moved to community-based approaches in the external portion of its supply chain.

In 2006, health care supply company Owens & Minor, a company based in Richmond, Virginia, with forty-six hundred employees and nearly $7 billion in revenue, found itself with a series of growing challenges. Developing new suppliers was a long, cumbersome process, and coordinating among suppliers and internal stakeholders needed significant improvement. Collaboration across individual elements of the supply chain was a related ongoing concern. Owens & Minor had to address these issues with new approaches while sustaining operations in a high-volume, low-margin business. In 2006, it acquired a major new line of business from a key competitor, requiring a major supply chain overhaul in order to complete integration.[6]

The solution was a familiar one: implementation of community-based supply chain management tools that were more open, transparent, collaborative, and self-service. However, instead of slavishly copying consumer social media, Owens & Minor ended up selecting a product from a company named RollStream that had taken many ideas from social media and online communities, including ease of use, user profiles, document and media sharing, and activity streams, and had crafted them into a working supply chain management tool that is highly social and collaborative and provides a high degree of visibility across supply chains through social media–style information sharing.

Within six weeks, with a new, much lower-barrier workflow for new suppliers, over 220 suppliers had made a successful transition to the new community-based supply chain environment. Suppliers could now enter the community, share files securely, find relevant contacts inside Owens & Minor, and communicate with the company about supply chain status. Perhaps most important, there was broader visibility across all supplier communications within the company. When a supplier said something in the supply chain community, everyone inside Owens & Minor saw it at the same time. Everyone could finally operate and make decisions with the same information because it came from the supplier in a synchronized fashion. The new social supply chain soon had a serious test: a new distribution center in New Mexico suddenly needed to come online quickly, having over four hundred additional suppliers to coordinate and funnel their products through the center effectively. Owens & Minor scrambled to put the new social supply chain environment to work. Because of self-service, ease of use, and smoother collaboration with the new suppliers, outreach and supplier setup were completed in less than a day—an impossible task with the old supply chain.

The Owens & Minor social supply chain demonstrates the effectiveness of adapting social media concepts to specific types of business activities instead of trying to adapt those activities entirely to social media. The results of applying the tenets of social business—create shared value by default, eliminate barriers to participation, engage the right community—on top of a business-specific solution was more effective and supportive of the new vision. Second, it showed how social media can be used effectively for all sizes of B2B companies. All organizations can benefit by allowing employees to tap directly into a current flow of information, enabling better decision making with the best and most up-to-date information at hand. Information becomes easily discoverable, flows naturally to where it's needed, informs others after the fact, and helps coordinate everyone who is involved without the need for additional overhead.

The Owens & Minor example shows the impact of redesigning the way a process works, incorporating social media directly into the way the business goes about its daily activities. This leads to another social business tenet, one that complements tenet 3: focusing on business outcomes for social media:

Social Business Tenet #10
The most effective social business activities are deeply integrated into the flow of work.

Naturally a good portion of social business involves general-purpose conversation and collaboration that isn't tied directly to a particular business process. In fact, three primary types of social business activity exist: ad hoc, process oriented, and content oriented (see Figure 10.1).

These activities, which we address in detail in later chapters, give insight as to what B2B activities may best be addressed by tenet 10. Ad hoc activities consist of unplanned or informal communication and work and in a B2B setting may be simple social interactions between two companies as they seek high-level information or get to know one another. These are less likely to benefit from a focus on tenet 10. However, more process-oriented, and to a lesser

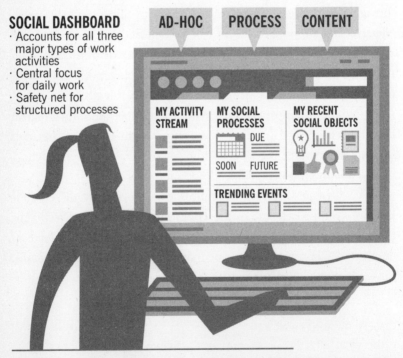

Figure 10.1 Three Major Types of Social Business Activity: Ad Hoc, Process Oriented, and Content Oriented

extent content-oriented, social business activities are ideal for deeper integration into the flow of work. Many organizations keep their systems of record (IT systems that do the heavy lifting when it comes to record keeping and transactions) separate from their systems of engagement, which include e-mail, phones, and social media. Owens & Minor's overhaul of its B2B supply chain to a more social model demonstrates clearly that when organization brings both systems of record and systems of engagement together in the full context of the work process, improved results are more likely by making work processes and flows of information more open, shared, and participative.

THE B2B SOCIAL BUSINESS OPTIONS

This wide range of representative B2B social business stories, from Microsoft and Owens & Minor to American Express and L'Oreal, shows a spectrum of social business partner approaches, along with a clear story that social media can be used to improve many aspects of the B2B business partner engagement and management process. At the leading edge, such as with the reinvention of information flow across the supply chain, social business paints a picture of how to begin the transformation to new modes of operation with trading partners that provide results impossible to achieve in any other way. Social business has been successful at driving improvements in the B2B aspects of partner support (Microsoft, L'Oreal), customer relationship management (American Express), and supply chain management (Owens & Minor). This then begins to paint the picture of what B2B social business looks like and consists of (see Figure 10.2).

B2B social business tends to be a bit more structured than some other types of social business approaches, such as social media marketing. The goal, at least in the examples that exist so far, is to improve specific and often very transactional activities such as overcoming barriers to product development, fixing problems in the supply chain, or getting support for a specific service issue. Relationships between companies are established for a particular purpose

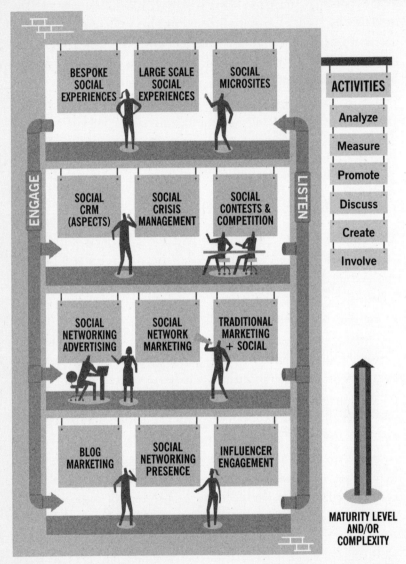

Figure 10.2 Examples of How to Use Social Business for B2B Engagement

rather than just general flows of communication or collaboration. In terms of the ways that social business can be employed to improve B2B outcomes, generally there are at least seven major applications, which we explore in the following sections.

Innovation Communities

Over time, most companies reach their natural limit on the pace of innovation, while at the same time a series of long-standing product development or R&D barriers goes unsolved. Without a major change to innovation inputs or business situations giving rise to unresolved R&D obstacles, companies are prevented from providing customers with a sustainable, ongoing set of evolving products and services. This can have serious consequences over time and may ultimately lead to disruption as competitors provide solutions to the shortcomings or obsolescence of a company's product line. In fact, companies will try to preserve the problem to which they are a solution and will tend to preserve the thinking that the problem promotes rather than plan for inevitable change.[7]

Companies can use new social business methods to leave their innovation challenges behind and help break the R&D logjams in their organization. Innovation communities can help, such as those offered by companies like enterprise innovation provider InnoCentive. Based outside Boston, the company has used its expert community, known as Solvers, to tackle more than thirteen hundred challenges across industries including agriculture, life sciences, and high tech using a social business platform that connects companies with socially shared ideas. When companies want to tap into a deep pool of innovation, they can issue a challenge to InnoCentive's Solver community with an award for successful completion, usually between $10,000 and $100,000.

In November 2006, InnoCentive's community tackled a long-standing problem of tracking amyotrophic lateral sclerosis (ALS), also known as Lou Gehrig's disease. An organization called Prize4Life offered a $1 million prize to anyone who could provide a means of measuring the progression of the disease, which would be instrumental in helping to discover a cure. An inexpensive, easy-to-use tool that could accurately track disease advancement in patients would make clinical trials of ALS drugs cheaper, faster, and far more efficient. A solution to this difficult problem had eluded the biomedical industry for decades. The InnoCentive community took six years and the combined efforts of over a thousand Solvers from twenty countries to work diligently to find a solution.[8] Ultimately Dr. Seward Rutkove developed a novel technique, electrical impedance myography (EIM), that sensitively measures the flow of tiny electrical currents through muscle tissue. Electric current travels differently through tissue depending on whether it's healthy or affected by ALS; by comparing the size and speed of electrical signals, EIM can accurately measure the progression of the disease. Rutkove later noted that without the effort of the community-based innovation effort by Prize4Life and InnoCentive, it's unlikely a solution would have resulted.

Open innovation can occur in many ways, and the one illustrated here is to tap into focused communities. This highlights a couple of key social business tenets central to the success of this B2B approach: tenet 1 (allow as many people as possible to participate) and tenet 5 (engage the right community for the business purpose).

Products as Open Community Platforms

Another way that companies can apply social business to drive forward R&D and innovation is to foster community much closer to their organization instead of using external communities like InnoCentive. Organizations encountering difficult problems have cultivated collaboration communities, sharing business information and opening processes to collaborate on solutions. To succeed, a company has to open up its internal supply chain to outsiders, typically by providing controlled, secure access to information and processes. It must also enlist and motivate a community of participants to help them solve the challenge at hand.

One example is the Goldcorp Challenge, where Goldcorp, a Canadian mining firm, was having difficulty finding more gold to prospect on its fifty-five thousand acres in Ontario. In literal desperation, it opened up all 400 megabytes of its valuable prospecting data to the geological community for help. Despite worries about loss of secrecy and looking foolish for not finding it themselves, they offered $575,000 in prize money for successful recommendations. More than one thousand entities from over fifty countries applied unique and highly disparate methods to crunching the data, including applied math, advanced physics, computer visualization, and many other creative methods. The success rate was impressive: over 80 percent of the new targets provided from the community yielded useful finds. Ultimately the challenge unearthed 8 million ounces of gold and catapulted the organization from a poorly performing company worth a mere $100 million into a $9 billion mining giant in a few years.[9]

A similar example comes from the highly competitive field of drug development. Pharmaceutical multinational GlaxoSmithKline (GSK) realized that large, internal R&D efforts were costly and often failed. R&D was more productive in smaller, more entrepreneurial environments, outside the cost structures and management overhead of a very large company.[10] The company needed to mitigate the high-stakes risks of new drug development while better tapping a vast global knowledge base to drive innovation.[11] GSK soon decided to launch a collaborative drug discovery initiative that would be entirely facing outward, with no internal drug development work of its own to manage; this community of B2B partners would be the sole source of new drugs in this model, and GSK could provide access to specialists, screening tools, and genetic databases, as well as help cooperatively bring new products to market.

The offshoot, known as Scinovo, steadily built its own community around the company, primarily a mix of small and midsized pharmaceutical companies and academic institutions. The result is a highly decentralized community process aimed at creating an effective pipeline of useful new drug compounds. Scinovo itself consists of a small community management and facilitation team that contributes to GSK entirely through the efforts of the community that it has built and no other source. The Scinovo effort has received a great deal of interest and scrutiny in the industry because it's a complete inversion of the process of traditional drug development, harvesting its community for useful ideas and then leveraging GSK's considerable global resources to deliver new products to market. Scinovo holds results close to the vest, but one of its partners, medicinal chemistry firm Ranbaxy Pharmaceuticals Canada, achieved a significant landmark by getting a breakthrough compound for respiratory inflammation into clinical trials. The result will be that GSK will acquire a powerful new drug to treat chronic obstructive pulmonary disease and Ranbaxy could ultimately receive $100 million in milestone payments for developing the drug in community partnership, as well as double-digit royalties.

The key to success for both Goldcorp and GSK was the realization that they had fundamentally limited innovation resources compared to the total knowledge possessed by those inside their industry as well as beyond and then opening up through the use of open community platforms. Success required the willingness to change expectations of how business gets accomplished, who does it, and how to collaborate in fundamentally new ways.

Partner Amplifiers

This approach works particularly well when a large company has a great number of smaller companies it must support. Offering traditional in-person representatives or even call centers to provide the often sustained and in-depth support required is a major challenge for companies that depend heavily on value chain partners to sell their products and services. The L'Oreal example illustrates a solution equally applicable to insurance agents, hotel franchises, e-commerce affiliates, and any other relationship where B2B collaboration must occur for the business relationship to realize effective results, such as increased sales in the channel and better customer acquisition and retention. Social business amplifies partner activities by driving network effects and other ecosystem benefits, such as having an organization come together with all of its partner companies to market, sell, innovate, support, or otherwise accomplish business objectives.

As in all social business, technology can be a key enabler for success, such as the tools that L'Oreal made available to its salons, but it's not required, as GSK's collaborative innovation program demonstrated. The program largely avoided traditional social media, but its actual processes and business model hewed directly to the key tenets of social business, making it possible for external innovators to have their drug development efforts amplified through the collaborative process with GSK. This is a key point worth repeating: social business is people-centric and can be supported by effective technology as long as the tenets are followed, but social media technologies themselves, though helpful in most cases, are not absolutely necessary to achieve usable results.

Affiliate and Partner Portals and Communities

These are private online communities designed just for B2B purposes and may be restricted given the types of proprietary information that is often exchanged in them. The SAP Community Network and American Express OPEN Forum are key examples of this approach. They are typically not focused on a specific type of transaction (like customer support cases) or business outcome (R&D or marketing), but instead allow the community to self-organize in a more general way to do all of these things. Affiliate and partner portals and communities produce emergent outcomes, and benefits cluster around whatever collaborative subjects companies in them choose to focus on. There are two primary participative models: point-to-point, where members can interact only with the business that created the portal, and networked, where members can largely see and interact with everyone in the community (see Figure 10.3). While point-to-point gives the portal's owner more control, it largely eliminates the possibility of useful self-organized outcomes. The networked model

POINT-TO-POINT   **NETWORKED**

Participants (outside) can   All participants can
only intereact with the   see and interact
company itself (center).   with each other.
· Not emergent   · Emergent
· Less self-organizing   · Self-organizing
· Less autonomous   · Autonomous

Figure 10.3   Outcomes of Point-to-Point Portals Versus Networked
Communities

is far preferable for results as long as privacy or regulatory issues prevent it from being used. Unfortunately, most organizations still largely provide B2B self-service portals that miss the networked social business opportunity of communities of participants to drive improved innovation, marketing, sales, support, and operations.

Social CRM

B2B social CRM can consist of a range of activities, from small scale to large, that generally has an effect in direct proportion to its intrinsic usefulness to participants and the size of the community that's engaged (tenet 4). A company doesn't necessarily have to build its own community or even make a large investment such as was required to build something with the quality and scope of the SAP Community Network. A popular way to support customers in social media is to watch their concerns being expressed in places like Twitter and engage with them as soon as issues arise.

This is exactly what Fortune 100 technology firm HP did for small business customers, creating a Twitter account, @HPBizAnswers, connected to the HP Business Answers blog to spread support information (along the way transitioning from local social media to external social media; see Figure 6.2) and complement discussions about small business use of its technology taking place across various outlets.[12]

For a more strategic use of B2B social CRM, Pitney Bowes turned to social media in order to reduce the ten dollar average cost to handle each customer support call it received in 2009. A large postal rate change took effect, causing a major rise in calls to the company's business support center, eventually exceeding 400,000 incidents. The company determined that social support was one of the few solutions that could provide a dramatic reduction in call center costs.[13] It quickly developed a B2B social CRM site and connected it to the main Web site so customers could easily locate the resource and search for answers there instead of contacting the call center. The typical pattern of social support ensued: users began helping like-minded users, who could build up reputation scores through user feedback and "best answers" tags. The savings Pitney Bowes gained from the biggest month of customer service engagement was more than double the annual cost of the social CRM service itself.

Social Supply Chains

Social supply chains offer new ways to engage processes, method-ologies, tools, and delivery models of a company's supply chain management efforts. The limited scope and slow pace of enter-prise supply chains pose growing challenges for organizations trying to balance the complex equations that govern and guarantee the healthy operation, growth, and evolution of increasingly dispersed businesses. Supply chain challenges are increasing due to intense global competition, rapid price and currency fluctuations, rising energy and transportation costs, short product shelf lives, demand for mass customization, offshoring, and talent scarcity. Applied well, social supply chains can offer compelling new solutions to many supply chain challenges for the following reasons:

• *Tapping into and making use of social networks that have deep reach across the organization's supply chain domain expertise.* These can enable major structural and operational improvements by collecting and tapping into the collective intelligence needed to meet both day-to-day and strategic-level supply chain requirements. This is what happened with Teva Pharmaceutical and, to a lesser extent, Owens & Minor.

• *Real-time social supply chain sourcing and self-service support.* Similar to the Goldcorp and GlaxoSmithKline examples, new open B2B supply chain services can be activated by business customers in real time to solve problems dynamically and effectively. A partner wants to get connected into the supply chain? Let it do the work and accelerate setup and establishment by self-service. Need to create a supply chain in a day? Connecting distribution and fulfillment systems of two or three new partners is short work if they have open supply chains. The future of supply chains lies in this model as enterprise ecosystems made up of partner communities and novel new network coordination systems take root.

• *Social exception management will become standard.* This was how Teva could quickly resolve supply chain issues: anyone in the supply chain can raise the alarm in social channels for all to see. Problem reports propagate by a social supply chain instrumented across the entire organization and optionally by suppliers, allowing rapid response. Microblogs on the assembly line or the distribution channel are often the start of this process for many organizations. Other key capabilities include social search (to find situations) and analytics (to understand the trends) and other tools to surface knowledge used to meet emerging challenges and needs.

• *The social supply chain becomes a profit center and a line of business in its own right.* Most companies are not yet ready to develop their own internal supply chain or engage the broader business world in the way that open supply chains from companies like Amazon, eBay, Best Buy, and World Bank have pioneered to considerable success. This is perhaps the most strategic of B2B social business applications. Social supply chains intersect with open supply chain as a method for engaging with the broadest partner set working with an organization's open supply chains. This is the only approach that scales cost-effectively and doesn't restrict growth due to relationship overhead and support requirements of many partners wishing to onboard themselves.

Open Supply Chain

Closely related to social supply chains, open supply chains represent the process of systematically opening up and connecting to a partner supply chain directly by self-service means. If two suppliers want to connect their inventory and shipping systems or communicate across their enterprise resource planning infrastructure, the process used to involve heavyweight integration. With open supply chains, the information portion of supply chains is laid open to partners using a simple set of technologies; the partners then connect themselves to a shared set of the company's data using self-service. While this was attempted in the days of electronic data interchange and other large-scale enterprise technologies, this new incarnation is significantly different, incorporating community-based approaches to engage and support participating business partners. In this manner, open supply chains combined with social supply chains support a set of highly complementary social business strategies. However, this aspect of B2B social business has been adopted largely only by Internet firms and Web start-ups, although this is beginning to change.

ASSESSING THE B2B SOCIAL BUSINESS ADVANTAGE

The most widely publicized success stories of social business hail primarily from the business-to-customer domain. There has long been a perception that relationships between businesses were an order of magnitude, or two or three times smaller than the relationships between business and consumers, leading to the conclusion that businesses may not have enough participants to achieve high levels of network effects. Social business technologies enable scale and distribute workloads to the edge of the network instead of doing everything centrally as in the past, driving meaningful benefits in B2B contexts. B2B social business is not only viable; it can be strategic in most of the many ways in which it can be employed.

The case examples in this chapter show the applicability of social media to B2B, as businesses are made up of people. Those people end up representing a large enough number to make an effective difference when redesigning who, where, and how productive capacity is made of social ecosystems. Given the importance of employees within social business, our focus now turns to workforce engagement and the connected company.

Chapter 11

Workforce Engagement

Creating a Connected Company Using Social Business

In 2006, Harvard professor Andrew McAfee heard from his students and elsewhere that a handful of forward-thinking organizations were using social media to make it easier to work together and facilitate collaboration. Social media were still relatively unknown beyond technology circles, and most adopters used existing tools for personal reasons. Although these efforts were early and often highly experimental, they hinted at possibilities of how these media could be used within organizations. Social media were bound to make their way into businesses if its application could improve information sharing, enable collaboration, and help retain knowledge where it could be easily found and reused by all.

McAfee explored a few early examples of social media in the workplace and wrote a groundbreaking treatise that laid out both its premise and promise: "Do we finally have the right technologies for knowledge work? Wikis, blogs, group-messaging software, and the like can make a corporate intranet into a constantly changing structure built by distributed, autonomous peers—a collaborative platform that reflects the way work really gets done."[1] McAfee called this new way of getting work done through social media "Enterprise 2.0," which focused primarily on the collab-orative, team-based activities that took place between employees internally. This started what has grown to be a wide-ranging trend as companies carefully—and not so intentionally or carefully in some cases—figure out how to incorporate the social communication innovations coming from the Web to their organizations.

Large organizations have operationalized Enterprise 2.0 princi-ples to improve workforce engagement, reshaping themselves into social businesses. The stories of IBM, MillerCoors, and Mountain Equipment Co-Op earlier in this book provide three examples. Another example comes from the use of wikis, user-editable Web pages. The power of wikis may be familiar to anyone who's used Wikipedia, but not as many people know why wikis are such potent tools. Wikis were invented by Ward Cunningham in the early days of the Internet, and it took a while for their core idea to catch on: that anyone can visit a wiki page and edit the information it contains. That's the general principle behind Wikipedia and why wikis follow the core tenet of social business: as many people as possible should be enabled to participate.

Morgan Stanley is a massive firm, with six hundred offices in the Americas, Europe, and Asia and 2011 net revenue of $32.4 billion. Social media, if applicable, would have to function inside this complex and highly sophisticated global environment. In 2004, an open source product called TWiki seemed to work well for the early adopters in the company's information technology department. Since it was easy to put information up on the intranet for all to see, the Morgan Stanley Twiki environment experienced rapid uptake, compared to the time-consuming processes required to go through traditional intranet content posting processes.

Wiki use quickly spread around the world for a multitude of uses, including vital services and process documentation, operations manuals, and collaborative team work spaces. Use increased such that by 2007, support had to be reconfigured to maintain multi-ple instances running on three continents; by 2011, over 500,000 topics existed in the Morgan Stanley wiki environment, with over 4 million pages viewed per month. Over half of the company's approximately sixty thousand worldwide employees use wikis every month to obtain information and update the company's global knowledge base. The accumulated information in the environment has grown to 350 billion characters.[2] Wikis enable the first two tenets of social business, while the structure and processes that surround it can enable the rest of them. Morgan Stanley has achieved a global social business transformation in the way it communicates and collaborates around knowledge workers, enabling every employee to contribute value as well as tap into it.

First identified as a growing trend in 2006, social business workforce engagement (or Enterprise 2.0) has an active role in many large and small organizations. Research firm Forrester pegged the number of companies investing in social tools to improve workforce collaboration at 42 percent in 2011.[3] For many, however, the objectives of workforce engagement and its processes are unclear, so it's worth examining how social business in the workplace happens and how it can create a more connected company.

THE ELEMENTS OF SOCIAL WORKFORCE ENGAGEMENT

Successfully enabling social media in the workplace requires a couple of key prerequisites: knowing what will be improved by the effort and defining success in terms that make sense from a traditional business perspective. Social business benefits accrue in many interesting but often unexpected places, and trying to figure out what these undefined outcomes are ahead of time is largely a fruitless exercise. Instead, companies should begin by solving a small set of well-defined business problems with social business solutions. Over time, emergent and highly opportunistic new local solutions to the existing problem—as well as, over time, emergent solutions to a host of downstream situations—will appear.

Blogs, wikis, microblogging tools, and an ever expanding set of social business suites attempt to provide social environments within which workers can engage and create improved business outcomes. 'We firmly believe that although social media are convenient and useful for social business, they are not the only option. Furthermore, consumer social media frequently cannot address the full range of capabilities that businesses need. Consequently, a practical understanding of social business in the workforce requires a step back to consider two foundational questions: (1) What exactly does *social* mean in the context of the social business tenets? and (2) What are the essential functions of an effective social business workforce environment?'

WHAT THEN *IS* SOCIAL?

Everything these days receives the label of "social" as long as sharing or communication is enabled in some way. There is some connection: e-mail is certainly social, as are mobile phones, and in fact most legacy communication technologies are social in some way. So what's the difference?

First, let's look at what exactly makes social media social, and then we'll look at social business to see if it's different. Structurally two fundamental aspects must be present for something to be considered social media:

- *The social graph.* This consists of a user profile that identifies a person and, optionally (but typically), a list of everyone that person is connected with. In other words, it's who a person is and those others he or she knows.
- *The activity stream.* This lists the events taking place between the social graphs of users. These are typically status updates or other messages, such as pictures or other media, that a person posts and are then visible to everyone listed as a social graph connection. It other words, it's a list of everything that's ever happened in terms

of sharing, communicating, and collaborating socially. Activity streams can take the familiar form of a Facebook feed or an orthogonal view of the most recent edit of a wiki page, which is still in an activity stream but one in which only the most recent activity is seen.

Those two components make social media social, along with a process to govern the participation process, where everyone can contribute and contributions automatically become visible to everyone in the social graph (as opposed to point-to-point, as in older communication methods). This goes to the heart of the key difference between traditional communication methods and social media: because created value is shared as widely as possible by default, social media enrich the entire community instead of a few narrowly defined interlocutors, based on network effects, that is, situations where each user in an environment creates value for others; more participants in a network create greater value for everyone involved.

Bob Metcalfe, the creator of Ethernet, the first workable computer network, saw the implications soon after he invented it: the value of networks is exponential due to the proliferation of the number of potential connections between nodes. He called it Metcalfe's law.[4] Thus, a million-person telephone network can theoretically connect all 1 million people to each other, though that never actually happens. In fact, most networks greatly underdeliver on the potential of deep connectedness. This relatively low level of use continued for several decades, until researcher David Reed began to validate what was different about social media. He asserted, and validated to a considerable extent, that the utility of large networks, particularly social networks, scales exponentially with the size of the network.[5]

However, by the time this insight emerged into collective consciousness, the world had largely discovered that social media were taking over global communication in the form of social networks. Social networks brought people together and facilitated communication, creating observable value for individuals.

The aggregation of individuals into groups led to the terminology of *social media:* open, shared participation in the context of that user's connections with others that results in high levels of shared value (the network effect).

As companies felt the impact of these trends, businesses began to consider commercial applications. Would the same ideas work and create value within business contexts as well? In social media, an environment must allow some sort of social graph and, for information to be distributed to user connections, some form of activity stream, in a way in which anyone's contribution can be viewed by all of that person's connections. Businesses create sharing environments with the intent of solving challenges to create value. Thus we arrive at a definition of *social business:* open, shared participation that results in high levels of shared business value (the network effect).

"Social business" can be a placeholder for "social media for business-related outcomes," but it also encompasses other forms of mass participation. For the workforce, this means that social business inside organizations encompasses a broader range of activities than might be found if the conception is limited to the notion of what consumer social media bring to the table (Figure 11.1).

Most companies approach workforce engagement by functional area, considering employee activities and workplace functions and then determining how processes could be improved by applying social media tools. Because so many communication methods exist, one of the signature challenges of social business design is detangling and reconciling the large palette of options in a way that is effective, nondisruptive, and compelling enough to get workers to change their behavior and do their work differently and more socially. There are a number of combinations of existing business systems and social media, but the functions that follow are the major types that organizations will have to consider and sort out into a clear, concise internal social business strategy that is supported by fundamental social media capabilities.

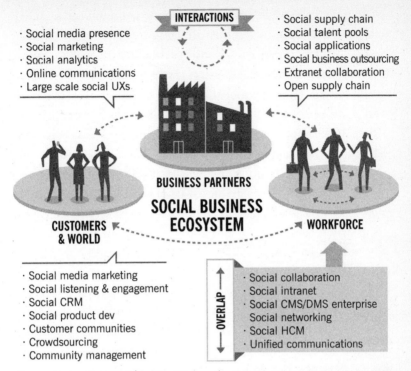

Figure 11.1   Connecting Workforce Engagement with the Full Vision of Social Business

Note: UX = user experience; CMS/DMS = content management systems/document management systems; HCM = human capital management.

FUNCTIONS OF WORKFORCE COLLABORATION

Social Collaboration

.1Also known as Enterprise 2.0, this is one of the most frequent starting points for those who are setting out to improve the performance of knowledge workers in the enterprise, typically the most valuable and important contributors in the organization. They are the decision makers, gatherers of strategic insight, and managers of the projects, the operations, and the direction of the company. Most companies already use collaboration tools ranging from SharePoint, e-mail, and instant messaging to videoconferencing and unified communication suites. Social collaboration tools put the social graph and activity streams in the center of the work process, becoming a dashboard for collaboration. The resulting environment connects to other frequently used communication systems to send notifications and reach users who otherwise haven't switched over to the social collaboration environment.

Social collaboration solutions can focus in two areas: horizontal collaboration that applies to any type of internal teamwork and process-specific collaboration enabling a halo of conversation to form around routine business activities. Making both work necessitates design into workflow and not requiring an extra system that users have to switch between.

Social Intranet

The intranets inside company networks have long been a target of criticism for being frequently out of date and difficult for workers to add or update information. Yet the corporate intranet has always had potential as a sort of miniature private Internet containing the sum of an organization's tacit knowledge, ongoing work, and useful reference information. However, it would be fair to say that the majority of intranets are relatively unsuccessful and typically see light use other than as a convenient reference point for human resource policy or for driving directions to corporate headquarters.

The formal processes of publishing and content management that most intranets impose on contributors also don't work very well for the give-and-take of freeform collaboration. Consider the origins of Wikipedia, which started out with a change management process for adding updates similar to corporate intranets. Wikipedia was initially part of Nupedia, a project to produce a free online encyclopedia. Nupedia employed a qualified, carefully screened group of expert contributors and a sophisticated multistep peer review process for new submissions. Despite its mailing list of interested editors and the presence of a full-time editor, the production of content using the centralized and bureaucratic process was extremely slow: after a full year of effort, only twelve articles had been produced. To facilitate production, a wiki was established to run parallel to Nupedia; it opened on January 10, 2001.[6] Within a month, over a thousand new articles had been posted. Studies have also subsequently validated that centrally produced work has similar rates of error as peer-produced work, and the latter are usually orders of magnitude richer and more diverse.[7] However, intranets at most organizations remain at the Nupedia level of capability.

Social Content and Document Management

Content and document management is a core activity of organizations and one of the most frequent tasks of today's information-intensive knowledge workers. This work has given rise to a generation of sophisticated and complex products designed to structure and control the production of business content, such as forms, paperwork, reports, spreadsheets, and scanned images. Systems keep track of the different versions, make them secure, organize them, help people find existing information, create paperwork trails, and connect everything to business work flows. In practice, most content management systems (CMS) and document management systems (DMS) ignore the key tenets of social business: they limit who can participate, are complex and hard to use thereby reducing participation, and so overly structure the process that they are often inconvenient to use.

Social CMS and DMS tools have emerged, although they do not always obey social business tenets. While some processes must by definition have limited access and be structured to meet certain requirements, most rules are greatly overdone. As an ideal model for participation, social media have shown that simple rules work best: radically simple usability, as little structure as possible, and open contribution. Reconciling CMS and DMS with social business requires a new look at the technologies being used, as well as a rethinking of how they are applied to the business.

Enterprise Social Networking

It's safe to say that most workplaces will receive an enterprise social network in the next few years. Some of these networks will see limited use, while others will be vibrant and strategic assets for how the company gets work done. Overlapping with the social collaboration and social intranet functions in this list, enterprise social networks are often considered in isolation, as a feature to be added to the network and not deeply connected to other business systems.

A more cohesive social strategy is needed to take into account and sort out the many social capabilities flowing into today's organizations. At its core, an enterprise social network looks a lot like an employee-only, single-company version of Facebook, though it's not usually visible to those outside the company. It can play a role in building cohesion among far-flung workers, locating expertise on the fly.

Social Human Capital Management

One unique area for social business in the workplace is in human resources (HR), which has long concerned itself with hiring and firing and more recently has turned to cultivating the potential of a company's workers. This includes the establishment of personal and professional development programs and creating policies designed to promote better worker performance. The discipline of workforce performance improvement is better known as human capital management (HCM). Because the open environments of social business leave behind a wealth of knowledge available on the network for all to see, discover, analyze, and learn, there are numerous human capital management implications. Benefits include capturing and preserving the acquired subject matter experience of staff members in high-turnover workforces, creating training programs, and identifying educational and developmental needs, which happens naturally if employees are "working out loud" in internal social business environments. Many HR and HCM products are beginning to incorporate social business approaches, creating opportunities while also increasing the growing challenge of social business fragmentation across so many business systems.

Unified Communications

For years, the proliferation of communication channels in the workplace, including e-mail, mobile phones, instant messaging, text messages, and video, made the process of consistently delivering and managing communication for workers a growing headache. Keeping track of all the contact points, making them available to workers, and shutting down channels efficiently on separation is an ongoing challenge for most organizations. The solution, unified communications, provides a single identity and set of tightly connected and consistent communication methods and contact points. Unfortunately, when social media came along, unified communications fell behind. Although this is not yet a major issue for most large organizations, reconciling unified communications with internal social business will be a growing priority for most Fortune 1000 companies.

KEY BENEFITS OF SOCIAL COLLABORATION

Fully enabled social businesses report a number of benefits:[8]

- *Better sharing of information.* Seventy percent of large companies see that the improvement in the level of information that appears is enabled by social business.
- *More direct information flows.* Information moves readily from those who have it and share it to where it is wanted and needed. Social networks are natural enablers of the viral propagation of needed knowledge, and workers can often find what they're looking for by search as long as that information has been shared. Fifty-five percent of large companies saw information routed around long-standing control points such as middle managers. This has important leadership and culture change implications that we explore later.

- *Collaboration across fiefdoms and silos.* Just over 40 percent of companies reported that workers connected better across organizational boundaries when engaging with each other using social business methods. The tenets of social business tend to encourage widespread participation from all corners of the organization. This is exhibited in the design of social media platforms and should also be reflected in the structure and process of the resulting social business solution.

- *Increased focus on project outcomes.* Many workers are notoriously focused on task-based activities to the exclusion of the big picture. Especially in large projects, even the most proactive workers can feel as if they are cogs without any visibility to the broader work taking place or how they affect it. With the open, transparent, and participative work environments of social business, employees can see the larger context and how their work fits in. Thirty-nine percent of organizations that use social business broadly saw a better focus on the results of project-scale efforts instead of individual tasking.

To limit the discussion to four benefits of internal social business is misleading, although the ones identified here are some of the more important ones. The benefits are extremely difficult to nail down because they are difficult to measure. The same is true with ways of working because their outcomes are many and varied.

The cause-and-effect chains, as they are called, are hard to get explicit credit for (see Figure 11.2), yet often have a significant impact on tangible financial outcomes.[9] In the end, many organizations will adopt social media as inevitably as they did e-mail, others will look at social business transformation of specific business processes where it's easier to do a more literal return on investment and usually see considerable value to be had, and still others will largely ignore the changes happening around them and not see the benefits until social business is a widely used approach. Therefore, the adoption narrative of social business in a given workplace will take many unexpected paths (tenet 6). A good example is seen in organizations

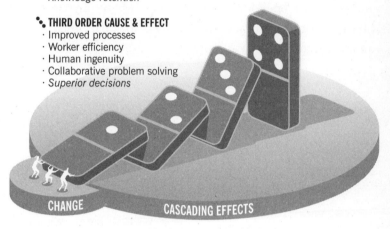

● **DIRECT CAUSE**
· Social networking
· Open knowledge management
· *Emergent collaboration*

✱ **SECOND ORDER CAUSE & EFFECT**
· Better discovery
· Cultivating weak ties/cross pollination
· Collective intelligence
· *Knowledge retention*

✱ **THIRD ORDER CAUSE & EFFECT**
· Improved processes
· Worker efficiency
· Human ingenuity
· Collaborative problem solving
· *Superior decisions*

∷ **FOURTH ORDER EFFECT**
· New products & services
· Increased profitability
· Higher quality work results
· Higher customer satisfaction
· Employee retention
· *More efficient operations*

CHANGE   CASCADING EFFECTS

Figure 11.2 Determining Social Business Value: Tracking Cause-and-Effect Chains

like Lloyd's Register, a leading global risk management firm based in London, where formal procedures were augmented in a dynamic way with social media to reduce the time taken to address customer queries.[10] Because social business activity can lead to many useful outcomes, these should be tracked and supported where they prove to be particularly promising to the business.

AN EXAMPLE OF A SOCIAL WORKFORCE

A good way to understand how social business works inside an organization is to look at an example that explores the activities and parts of the business affected. In Figure 11.3, a typical social business environment is shown with various actors as they go about their daily work. The principal output is the social work stream that continues to grow and get richer as everyone spends their day sharing, collaborating, and contributing knowledge. The environment is one or more social business tools, based on social media concepts, on the local intranet or elsewhere in existing information technology systems. At the bottom are typical line employees who work socially and out in the open with the processes, where anyone can look at their activity stream and even virtually look over their shoulder. Knowledge continues to accumulate from the full range of workers

Figure 11.3   An Example of Social Business in the Workplace

following their daily processes in the social business environment. Their team leaders and managers can keep better track of their progress and suggest changes early and often to drive more rapid course corrections and better agility, and executives can track all of this and have dashboards fed by analytics that allow all the open and observable work to be tracked and reported in real time, giving them a sense of the pulse of the organization.

To facilitate this orchestra of collaboration is a small team of what are known as community managers (we discuss their role in the next chapter), who are essential for maintaining the health and effectiveness of the social business environment, resolving problems, providing just-in-time solutions, providing social business skill building, and training, and much more. Just as an IT system needs a help desk, a social business needs community managers. Since the work proceeding across the company is open and visible, HR and legal can also ensure that social media policies are being followed and can provide oversight and assistance to workers who cross the line, intentionally or unintentionally. Subject matter experts (SMEs) within the company can be identified and plugged into processes quickly so work doesn't come to a halt without key information that's readily available somewhere else in the organization. External SMEs can be brought in to augment internal ones if necessary.

The result is a dynamic global activity stream containing everything the companies knows, who knows it, and what took place. The social work stream is the history of the organization and the narrative of nearly every process. It can be mined, analyzed, filtered, and processed for countless useful outcomes. Social business requires culture change, executive leadership, business process redesign, and technological updates to get to its full strength, but increasingly it's possible to get there in increments. The chapters in Part Three explore the process of social business design.

Chapter 12

Social Business Supporting Capabilities

You can get a sense of what is required to succeed with social business through the trials and experiments of early adopters. These hard-won lessons have provided key insights into the building blocks of social business success. We recommend the supporting capabilities explored in this chapter to maximize the outcomes and potential value created by social business strategy. Each has a critical role to play, and while early adopters achieved some measure of success without all of these capabilities in place, nearly all of them wished they had not omitted the investment in time and resources that these require. By exploring each in some detail, organizations will get a better sense of what's needed beyond the actual social business capability itself.

COMMUNITY MANAGEMENT: THE ESSENTIAL SOCIAL BUSINESS CAPABILITY

Consider the situation of a frustrated worker who wanted to create a secure place for his team to work collaboratively on the intranet but couldn't figure out how to create a space and verify it was secure.

He realized that the team should put its work out in the open for all to see and comment on, and they might eventually be able to do that, but the team was not quite there yet. He posted his unhappiness about this as a status update in his user profile on the company's internal social network. Surprisingly quickly and somewhat unexpectedly, a colleague responded with a social networking message identifying herself as a community manager and saying she was there to help him. She said her goal was to help him be successful at what he was trying to do. After briefly consulting with him, she went off and analyzed what the worker had done. She came back and said, "I see what you did and found the problem. I fixed it, and you and your team should be ready to work. Once you want to share this work more widely and need help, just let me know."

This example demonstrates the degree of facilitation that's required to make any social environment successful. One of the long-standing questions of social business has been how to support the activities of those within the collaboration environment and ensure they're being successful. The answer increasingly has become the discipline of community management. Community managers are the collaborative "X factor" who make communities work. One part evangelism, one part end user support, one part collaborative facilitation, and one part jack-of-all-trades, the community manager role has proven to be critical in ensuring social business success.

A comprehensive model mapping out roles and maturity levels in community management comes from the Community Roundtable (CR), the industry's leading source of practitioner lessons learned and effective practices. The CR defines four stages of maturity and eight competencies that must be mastered by organizations seeking to manage social business communities, whether internal or external to the company (Figure 12.1). The four stages of social business maturity break down like this:

Stage 1: Hierarchy. Little or no use of social business or community-based processes

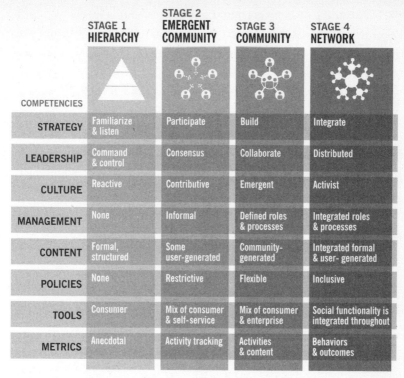

COMPETENCIES	STAGE 1 HIERARCHY	STAGE 2 EMERGENT COMMUNITY	STAGE 3 COMMUNITY	STAGE 4 NETWORK
STRATEGY	Familiarize & listen	Participate	Build	Integrate
LEADERSHIP	Command & control	Consensus	Collaborate	Distributed
CULTURE	Reactive	Contributive	Emergent	Activist
MANAGEMENT	None	Informal	Defined roles & processes	Integrated roles & processes
CONTENT	Formal, structured	Some user-generated	Community-generated	Integrated formal & user- generated
POLICIES	None	Restrictive	Flexible	Inclusive
TOOLS	Consumer	Mix of consumer & self-service	Mix of consumer & enterprise	Social functionality is integrated throughout
METRICS	Anecdotal	Activity tracking	Activities & content	Behaviors & outcomes

Figure 12.1 The Four Stages of Social Business Maturity and the Eight Competencies of Community Management

Source: Happe, R. "The Community Maturity Model." *Community Roundtable,* June 16, 2009. http://community-roundtable.com/2009/06/the-commu nity-maturity-model/.

Stage 2: Emergent community. Some experiments and early pilots of social business tools, processes, or online communities

Stage 3: Community. Well-defined, chartered, resourced, and staffed social business initiatives that have resulted in measurable business outcomes

Stage 4: Network. An integrated companywide social business strategy driven by a deep connected perspective inside and outside the organization

Community managers have complex roles and many responsibilities. Despite having the same title, external and internal community managers have very different jobs. External-facing individuals who primarily manage an organization's Facebook or Twitter presence or moderate owned communities as part of a marketing or corporate communications role are one type of community manager. Internal-facing individuals who work with colleagues trying to make the most of internal social networking environments are the other type of community manager. In both roles, community managers are involved

PLATFORM MANAGEMENT
· Upgrades
· Software know-how
· Feature selection

COMMUNITY MANAGEMENT
· Control / Management
· Moderation & rule enforcement
· Elicit participation
· Rewards & incentives

PROJECT MANAGEMENT
· Priority & schedule management
· Documentation

BRAND MANAGEMENT
· Brand support
· Situation management
· Capture brand feedback

CUSTOMER MANAGEMENT
· Outreach
· Events
· Incentives
· Issues management

SOCIAL BUSINESS COMMUNITY MANAGER

STAFF DEVELOPMENT
· Recruiting
· Team building
· Staff training

BUSINESS PLANNING
· Budgeting
· Goal definition
· Business alignment

PROFESSIONAL DEVELOPMENT
· Networking
· Identification of best practices
· Attend trade events

ADVERTISING & MARKETING
· Listen/join conversation
· Marketing analysis
· Impact reporting
· Ad rotation

PRODUCT MANAGEMENT
· Incorporator of experience
· Product selection

CONTENT MANAGEMENT
· Content plan
· Research & insight

Figure 12.2   The Social Business Community Manager: A Jack of All Trades

in a broad array of activities, ranging from customer management and content schedules to brand management and marketing support (see Figure 12.2).

The best community managers have a proactive customer service attitude, are highly supportive of their customers, and have a high level of emotional intelligence to work with the many types of workers, customers, and business partners they engage with while enabling social business. They also need to understand the business, often have technical expertise, and are well connected socially to draw participants together.

SOCIAL ANALYTICS AND BUSINESS INTELLIGENCE

The field of social analytics and resulting business intelligence applications has recently become a new supporting capability for effective and mature social business organizations. Three key realizations are driving widespread interest in social analytics by social business practitioners.

First, social media are rapidly becoming the richest new sources of new information. Most organizations have only recently realized that the Internet, the world's largest network, is already mostly peer produced. As a result, social media generate more information than any other source. As social business also becomes widely implemented inside most organizations, the same proliferation of information will happen. The information onslaught, while containing essential information, must be filtered and aggregated into a form that's usable, insightful, highly actionable, and strategic. Organizations will need upgraded analytics and business intelligence capabilities in order to make sense of the knowledge their competitors will also be mining for better market advantage.

Second, business intelligence must take into account the whole social business ecosystem. Merely examining a company's own internal databases or even the information that business partners have is no longer adequate to build an accurate picture of key events and trends that have important business impacts. Maintaining an integrated social business view today means connecting all internal business data with external information streams, with as little delay as possible. The challenge will be that social business data outside an organization also outnumber internal data by many orders of magnitude, so sifting through the synthesized whole to spot urgent situations and important issues quickly enough to drive business decisions is the objective.

Finally, organizations must cultivate new competencies to handle an effective social business listening and engagement process or risk disruption, irrelevance, or both. Most traditional analytics departments aren't yet highly skilled at processing social media, which requires connecting distributed conversations across hundreds of social networking services, tying in any associated rich media, and integrating with decentralized blog feeds and partner ecosystems. Most businesses also can't turn today's petabyte streams of raw information into usable strategic insight quickly enough to make a difference. Moreover, most business intelligence tools are not easy enough to use in order to have a significant impact on the business. One key competence, increasingly called big data, uses cutting-edge technologies to swallow the massive streams of data in social ecosystems and quickly sort through them for business advantage. The key to this is combining social analytics, which can deal with the unique aspects of social media, with big data, which can process vast, real-time information flows quickly enough to matter. The result is something that's sometimes referred to as social business intelligence (SBI).

The resulting real-time look into an organization's internal and external social business activities must be accurate, and there must be a means to verify it. It must be timely and comprehensive, because leaving anything out will likely result in a compromised analysis. And it must be comprehensible to the average worker in the organization, although this quality separates most social analytics capabilities from actual business intelligence, while the rest is what big data help bring to the table. But this shift to social business sources for key insights will still take some time. Classic business intelligence will remain essential for the foreseeable future to look into and understand what's inside an organization's systems of record, and a few tools will even move into social business intelligence. However, the larger shift today to systems of engagement as a primary—and even the majority—source of new business intelligence will almost certainly require fundamentally new types of social business intelligence tools based on new technologies so that workers can quickly access real-time filtered data and get the insight they need to perform their jobs.

There are at least two types of social business intelligence being developed. The first is the application of a social layer within traditional business intelligence tools to enable the collaboration and sharing of business intelligence by applying social media techniques. The second type, needed for long-term and sustainable social business and a healthy virtuous listening and engagement cycle, is the use of business intelligence tools with social media activity itself—both worldwide activity external to the organization and internal social workforce and business-to-business activities.

CORE SOCIAL BUSINESS INTELLIGENCE STRATEGIES

Although social analytics and business intelligence are only few years old as of this writing, effective business strategies for them have begun to emerge. For now, most organizations try to create basic social business intelligence capabilities and build experience with them. Some organizations have rapidly discovered that the level of effort needed and infrastructure required make "cloud-based" offerings (computing as a service, not a product) an easier path to usable results (at least in terms of time to market, feature set, and maturity), acquiring capability, and starting to experiment.

Thus, the choices are the usual ones: build, buy, or use the cloud. Regardless of what path is chosen, social business intelligence invariably consists of new data techniques combined with social analytics with a domain-specific business intelligence dashboard provided on top (see Figure 12.3). Once these social business intelligence capabilities are assembled, they enable the following strategies that will become competitive differentiators or drivers of additional efficiency and productivity:

- *Customer engagement and retention.* Simple social analytics provides an unfiltered data stream about what customers are doing in a company's social channels, understanding what action customers are taking that affect the organization and pointing out where best to engage by turning analytics into intelligence. Social listening services such as Radian6 have become leading examples of the capabilities in this space, rapidly developing social business intelligence features that lead to business-specific outcomes.
- *Social business adoption tracking.* Social analytics is invaluable for measuring the uptake of a social business effort. This ranges

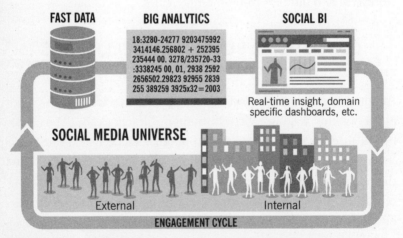

Figure 12.3 Turning Social Activity into Useful Business Intelligence

from measuring the viral uptake of external communities to identifying who is having trouble making the move to social channels and why.

- *Sales funnel analysis.* Sales teams have traditionally been a function driven by reports and numbers, but demand generation is increasingly zeroing in on social channels for building an inbound sales funnel. Social business intelligence can build an informative and detailed picture of what the funnel looks like in near real-time without time-consuming manual data collection and analysis. Examples of services providing tools to uncover these insights include traditional analytics providers like Adobe and start-ups including Kontagent.

- *Expertise and reputation tracking.* When connecting to the world and the workplace moves to activity streams, the people in them want to know if the information they see in their public social networks and social intranets is accurate and authoritative. Can the information be trusted, and is it right? Social business workers also want to be able to identify and keep track of influencers and experts. Social business intelligence can be used to build and manage the large data sets needed to enable solutions that can provide just these capabilities. Twikis, used in the Morgan Stanley case example, developed a new embedded reputation widget so that workers who don't know each other can get a community estimate of their reputation to evaluate their contributions with.[1] A more strategic example is from SAP Community network. SAP developed an internal people finder application that employs social analytics aimed at both external social media and internal social tools to find the right expert, just in time, for a given business situation using a custom-built mobile application.[2]

- *Human capital management.* Gaining insight into employee performance, identifying and tracking new talent to recruit, and a range of other key human capital management scenarios can be enabled with effective social business intelligence solutions. Companies like Taleo, SuccessFactors, and Rypple are increasingly offering deep social networking integration features for human resource functions like talent sourcing, performance management, and social business policy tracking.

- *Compliance and regulatory monitoring.* Organizations that operate in regulated industries or in countries with strict privacy laws need to know what their level of compliance with legal requirements is through constant tracking, analysis, and violation detection of social media activity within their organization and across the firewall. They'll use reporting and dashboards to understand as soon as a compliance issue has occurred, something that often takes natural language processing and machine learning techniques to determine. Companies such as Socialware are increasingly offering effective off-the-shelf solutions to make this more of a turn-key process available on demand.

- *Brand insight.* Brand monitoring is almost certainly more possible in social media than in just about any other medium, even though its use is still in the early adoption phase. Even basic monitoring, however, can require significant data capabilities. Monitoring alone isn't enough, and making sense of the vast streams of information that brand analysis can enable through visualization, reporting, and dashboards is where social business intelligence comes into the picture. Key examples of this include Visible Technologies' intelligence features, as well as the Dachis Group's Social Performance Monitor.

- *Social supply chain optimization.* The information shared in social supply chain platforms can be mined to provide a wide range of insights into exceptions, trends, and other key performance indicators.

- *Operations management.* Companies deploying internal social business solutions often find that as work processes open up and can be tracked in social media, the information in employees' activity streams can be used to power operational intelligence dashboards and reporting solutions.

SOCIAL BUSINESS IN REGULATED INDUSTRIES

Financial services, health care institutions, and the legal industry all have serious challenges with regulatory and compliance beyond the standard ones that any large company has, in particular public ones, in terms of engaging with the world through social business. Rules regarding records retention, patient confidentiality, and data discoverability, in addition to immature legal standards, create obstacles in using social media for external customer engagement. Even internally, compliance can be a challenge to deal with among a company's own workers. The obstacles that regulated industries face in working through their social business strategy can quickly turn into a seemingly insurmountable roadblock. But as more and more organizations in these industries have success stories to tell, a picture begins to emerge on what's required in order to succeed. These new capabilities—which are actually just best practices and lessons learned for the most part—make it possible for a large percentage of companies to make a transition to social business, which seemed almost impossible a few years ago.

The arrival of potent new support capabilities makes automated social business compliance and policy rule checking easy to implement. Affected organizations now have options that don't require them to build sophisticated capabilities or solve the many difficult problems with regulation and social media by themselves. This, then, is part of the answer on whether regulated firms will be able to engage in social business and use social data safely.

The specifics of how regulated businesses can engage in social business is becoming clearer. What these businesses need is a smart and agile approach to the definition, communication, and enforcement of enterprise social business policy. In this view, organizations don't have to do it all themselves; they can leverage the experiences of those that have gone before. Also, capable new solutions can enable automated and predictive processes that make much it less likely that the company will be exposed to risk from communication outside compliance guidelines and regulatory parameters.

Figure 12.4 sets out the key elements of a new vision for an operational and dynamic social media policy life cycle. By establishing the right compliance, analytics and reporting, and business rule layers in direct concert with a well-articulated and communicated social media policy, most regulated industries can move beyond regulatory and compliance hurdles and begin accessing the benefits of becoming a compliant social business.

The industry has begun to see the introduction of specialized services from social software vendors to realize a new vision for social media enablement—one that's driven by policy yet helps participants feel empowered to act as they need to and knowing they'll be kept within the prescribed regulatory, governance, and policy boundaries. When it comes to the strategies that enable access to social business

*Uncommon but highly effective inclusions

Figure 12.4   An Operational Social Media Policy Life Cycle

for companies worried about legal exposure, the best environment is one where social business actors across the company are free to create the collaborative patterns, structures, and processes they need to work together, inside, outside, or between companies. When they have an automated safety net, powered by social analytics that has been explained the policy restrictions, it ensures that workers can act with confidence and that access to social business transformation is once again possible. When corporate governance teams and senior executives come to understand that a safety net is operational at all times for all of the organization's social business activities and that it accurately represents their wishes and concerns, they have the confidence to begin driving social business objectives forward.

THE REGULATED SOCIAL BUSINESS LIFE CYCLE

Three major types of activities are required to deliver on social business in regulated industries:

- *Define social business policy.* The social media policy for all companies should be contained in a blog post, wiki page, or other social artifact so it can be readily accessed, updated quickly and simply, and commented on and discussed by workers so that a useful discussion ensues that drives improvements and organizational clarity. It should be updated after every significant lesson learned.
- *Communicate social business policy.* The social media policy must be communicated through training, by clearly articulated goals and incentives, and by executives who lead by example.
- *Verify social business policy.* New social media compliance tools can be used to operationalize and embody the social media policy as an actual, functional agent in the social business, creating secure narrative logs for regulators and internal audit, while monitoring social business conversations, detecting policy violations, and interceding on its own if necessary.

PART THREE

SOCIAL BUSINESS DESIGN AND STRATEGY

Chapter 13

Identifying Priorities and Planning

S tarting down the road of social business transformation requires, as one might expect, an effective plan. Although few plans involving significant innovations for an organization survive for long in their original form, social business projects typically benefit from a process that embraces change and makes rapid course corrections from early lessons learned. Organizations can even elect to employ social business methods in the business design process, opening them up using social media to a broad range of interested stakeholders across the company.

The first step is determining the business objectives of a social business strategy that, when followed, will lead to the desired outcomes. The objectives to be achieved by moving to social business should be captured from two essential sources. The first is the set of participants who will be involved—exclusively workers for internal social business improvements or a combination of workers and customers for a social customer relationship management effort or social marketing effort, or just a set of business partners for a business-to-business community. The second is the set of enterprise objectives, typically defined by the executive team, board of directors, and or other existing high-priority strategy efforts. The point of this process is to gather from the critical stakeholders a set of goals that are mutually aligned at an organizational level and in the broader context of the business and with the front lines of employee-to-customer interaction where work actually takes place and with the groups of people who will be directly involved.

First, however, it's worth briefly exploring the larger process of deliberately encouraging intentional and emergent change. Neither one nor the other alone will result in the kind of results most organizations are seeking or must achieve in order to see the results set out in the social business stories we have related in this book. Consequently, for the purposes of putting the techniques under a single rubric, this combined intentional process is sometimes referred to as *social business design*: that is, the process of intentionally transforming a business with social media through a well-defined, agile, and adaptive process so that both specific and emergent benefits result.

SOCIAL BUSINESS TRANSFORMATION: THE HIGH-LEVEL PROCESS

To put the requirements and the prioritization process in the full context of social business design, it's worth looking at the entire process, which forms the foundation of and is the goal of the concepts described in the chapters in Part Three. Posing the simple question, "What problem are we trying to solve?" can go a long way toward identifying the initial direction of a social business initiative; in addition, a brief introduction to the entire process is highly effective at the beginning of an exploration of this topic.

Figure 13.1 shows the entire process of social business design, along with the major resulting activities, change processes, and outcomes. At the center of this figure is the establishment of strategic goals and a road map that will be revisited regularly throughout the social business design process. Around this, in the center stack, are the elements of change that help support a far-reaching yet well-managed social business design process. Although we focus primarily

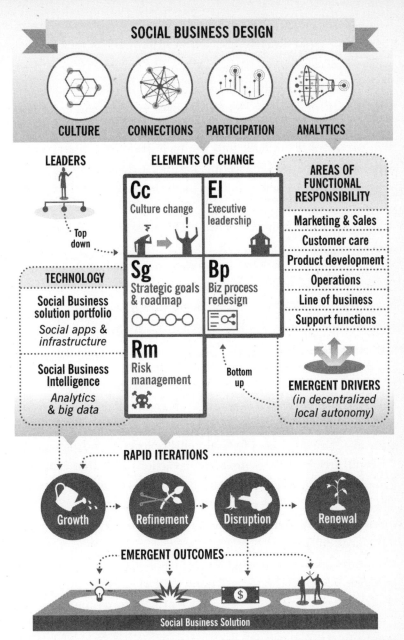

Figure 13.1 Applying Social Business Design for Organization-Wide Transformation

on this activity in this chapter, here is a breakdown of each of the key elements of social business design (we explore each of these in detail in Part Four):

- *Culture change.* Applying the ten tenets of social business requires a deft touch to drive the desired changes in organizational culture that define how work gets done. Encouraging workers to think about their processes and interactions as much more open, participative, and community based than in the past is the goal. Typically part of a social business change management program that's integrated into a targeted business process redesign effort, culture change is driven by a simultaneous effort of high-level leaders (executives and managers) in concert with a conscientious and dedicated community management team in carrying out a change management program. The companies that have achieved rapid adoption of social business (IBM, Mountain Equipment Co-Op), meaning that this affected more than a third of workers in a single year, engaged in this dual culture change process.

- *Executive leadership.* One of the earliest lessons learned when social business began appearing in the workplace was that the actions taken by internal leaders have a profound effect on adoption and positive outcomes. In fact, Andrew McAfee, in his original exploration of the early business users of social collaboration, found that success "depends greatly on decisions made and actions taken by managers."[1] This means that identifying internal champions among managers and executives is a key part of the early process. Cultivating their sponsorship, involvement, and even their participation can make a substantial difference.

- *Strategic goals and road map.* Clearly identifying and establishing the objectives of a social business strategy create a vision and provide the ingredients to build a description of how to get there, often a road map, which we explore in more detail in Chapter Sixteen. Once the goals of the strategy have been identified, at least the intentional ones, the process of determining priorities and planning, the focus of this chapter, for the entire strategy can begin.

- *Business process redesign.* Driving the results of a social business strategy requires that the process of applying it ends up changing the way the target organization or business processes operate. Some of these changes will be planned from the start, and others will be identified, evaluated, and either encouraged or discouraged depending on the criteria set by the strategy. Cultivating and managing for emergent change is discussed in Chapter Seventeen, and control and oversight over the process are covered in Chapter Eighteen.

- *Risk management.* For many organizations, the perceived risks of social business are significant concerns, particularly in regulated industries but also for global brands that are engaging externally. There is risk in both not acting, as when Toyota or BP inadequately responded through social media during their respective crises, and in acting in a way that exposes the organization to risk. A successful social business strategy spends due diligence on risk while not making it the focus of the effort.

- *Social business solutions.* Typically developing a social business strategy and matching social business design requires the introduction of new technologies. These are usually social media tools or infrastructure that provide necessary communication and collaboration capabilities. It can be general purpose and encompass the entire organization, or it can be focused on a particular function, such as customer care or product development, and affect only a department, responsibility, or function. (Any combination of these is also possible.) Most often companies select a social network, solutions that provide integration with security and identity standards, some external social media, and analytics tools. (The building blocks of social business are set out in Chapter Fourteen.)

- *Social business intelligence.* Guiding a social business strategy once social business capabilities are operational in the organization requires the ability to tap into and listen to the work taking place to glean the metrics, trends, and sentiment of the participants. This wealth of knowledge permits the social business effort to begin to manage what it is able to measure, invaluable for identifying not only areas encountering difficulties (such as low levels of effective collaboration) but also opportunities. Social business intelligence provides a window onto the activities of a community and can be used to measure effectiveness, return on investment, and key performance indicators that should align with the goals and priorities that have been established and kept updated.

At a high level, social business design (as pictured in the upper left of Figure 13.1) is the deliberate process of transforming the organization to social business and involves its existing culture, connections among all communities relevant to the organization, architectures of participation to engage constituents in useful outcomes (both intentional and emergent), and analytics that drive the process of improvement, management, governance, and risk. Structuring and enabling are the principal activities of a social business strategy. When these are done effectively, the results that the organizations described throughout this book have achieved are possible for most organizations. The outcomes (shown at the bottom of Figure 13.1) are the social business solutions, both planned and spontaneously discovered or created by the participants themselves, that achieve the shared and top-down goals of the organizations.

REVISITING PRIORITIES AND PLANNING

This examination of the process of social business transformation will help organizations better understand what planning for social business transformation entails. It must describe how the organization will apply social business design combined with the organization's commitment to realize the elements of change. Only this will result in a successful and least disruptive move to social business. Like SAP's Community Network and Procter & Gamble's Old Spice campaign, social business success was achieved through a clear set of objectives: better engagement and support of customers using complex products (for SAP) and updating a brand and improving sales (for Procter & Gamble).

It's usually not hard for companies to articulate interesting high-level social business objectives: a more useful and vibrant intranet, better marketing that's less expensive and more engaging, or tapping into better sources of innovation to solve long-standing business problems, for example. However, this is a limited view that largely accepts the existing ways of doing business. There is a more pervasive and far-reaching way of looking at social business transformation, which requires that many more assumptions are laid bare for reconsideration. How can we achieve business objectives by completely setting aside the old ways of conducting operations and directly plugging in the tenets of social business? The answer is by casting off notions of how work should proceed, who does it, and even what the economics should be; only then can sustained, meaningful, and effective transformation occur.

However, most organizations are not prepared to immediately engage in widespread and deeply affecting business transformation, no matter what the upside potential might be. It entails too much perceived risk, more change than the organization can handle in a short time, and many other reasons. Consequently, here are some key insights into planning a social business strategy and design effort:

• *Clearly identify goals, but don't assume how they'll be achieved.* Create an environment of strategic thinking about social business that never prescribes how solutions will be achieved. The social business design process will address this, but the planning process should not at first, as hard as that may be. This can be achieved most directly by changing how social business strategy goals are defined. For example, instead of, "Incorporate social media to cost-effectively amplify outbound marketing," phrase this as, "Employ social media to increase customer engagement levels while lowering costs." "Add social media to the intranet so that workers can more easily share information and collaborate" can be changed to, "Provide an environment where workers can more easily participate with each other and their stakeholders." "Improve customer care with an online self-help community" can be turned into, "Apply social media in new ways to increase customer satisfaction and lower support costs." Removing the how is key to ensuring that the thinking does not overly focus on the solution at first, which can contaminate thinking and limit outcomes. One lesson learned in many of the case examples presented in this book is that the first thing that's tried often needs to be followed up with a more experienced and informed solution.

• *Use a phased approach.* A social business strategy can easily encompass too much change by looking at the many areas of the business that can be improved with the use of social media. While some social business experts, including Andrew McAfee himself, advocate doing away with the use of a pilot process (arguing that it limits critical mass and participation, a topic explored in Chapter Fifteen), it's possible to try to accomplish too much too fast.[2] Getting the timing right and determining the successful rate of transformation are keys to achieving a balance that doesn't go too slow or too fast.

• *Understand that planning must continuously evolve.* Serendipity is one of the most startling outcomes of social business. While organizations can intentionally reach impressive outcomes that collapse costs and improve objective performance measures of specific business functions (such as Intuit's Live Community approach to customer support in Chapter Three), just as often a group of workers or customers, using the free-form platforms of self-expression they've been offered by the organization, will cobble together new processes, solutions, products, and outcomes. Beyond this, the social business strategy will also make numerous discoveries of its own because of social business intelligence and the fact that processes are much more open and observable than in the past, leading to insights that should be feedback into the planning process (shown as the rapid iterations in Figure 13.1) and resulting in updated goals and road map. The social business strategy, including the goals and road map, should be updated routinely—not just during the effort but as long as the organization engages in social business and wishes to guide the outcomes both deliberate and spontaneous.

- *Expect more frequent "disruption."* Classic business processes based on fixed, repeatable processes are giving way to more dynamic ones enabled by social business. Process flows and critical methods evolve more quickly with the rapid information flows of social media, as well as the introduction of new actors and stakeholders at a faster pace and from far-flung corners of the organization and even the rest of the world. The process of growth, refinement, disruption, and renewal (see Figure 13.1) is present in all business cycles, but it occurs much more rapidly with social business. Change is the norm, and the process explored here seeks to apply the proven results of agile methods to adapt to change more naturally and continuously.

The planning process should therefore consist of capturing business requirements in a way that the local organization is competent in using, while also expecting, and even encouraging, local solutions by those using the social media solutions they've been given in novel and useful new ways. Prioritization can be determined through dependency analysis, business urgency, cost and impact estimates, and other traditional measures, but they should be revisited as part of the overall replanning process. Because social business processes evolve and change quickly and with less deterministic outcomes, the transformation process is never complete. Although a social business design process has a definite beginning and end, at least for the deliberate outcomes, the social business transformation process never truly ends and can even creatively disrupt itself if the organization so desires.

Chapter 14

Building Blocks

The Elements of Social Business

Throughout this book, we have presented numerous stories of companies that have achieved outcomes that improved business performance by one measure or another. Each story focused on a certain capability of the business, such as marketing or customer care, and explored how social business approaches drove better business results. Along the way, we have set out certain tenets as root causes of the results these businesses achieved. To activate these tenets, social business design applies specific techniques and technologies to achieve desired alignment with downstream goals.

The palette of elements available to a social business strategist or designer needs definition. What approaches and tools can be brought to bear, and what are their known benefits, strengths, and weaknesses? Consumer and enterprise social media have become a vast panoply of services, platforms, technologies, standards, and tools. There are hundreds of consumer social networks and thousands of software tools and services, with options like hosted and on premises and open source or commercial. Market leaders can change with often dramatic alacrity. For example, one of the first mainstream social networks was MySpace, launched in 2003, but it was dominant for only a short period and was overtaken definitively by Facebook in April 2008.[1] Companies that had based their social business strategies around the unique audience and capabilities of MySpace experienced more impact than those that designed for a higher range of change and a higher-level concept of what they were seeking to achieve.

Fortunately, the broad outlines of core social business building blocks can be discerned. However, one more significant wrinkle must be considered: the nature of digital change itself, which is primarily concerned with how the Internet is used to conduct business. Therefore, it's somewhat difficult to consider many aspects of social business in a vacuum from an organization's overall digital strategy, such as Web presence, e-commerce, Internet advertising, online video, and search engine optimization. In fact, social media are increasingly pervading each aspect of these digital practices, making them more participative, social, and emergent.

Thus, this chapter focuses on examining the big picture of social business in relation to modern digital strategy, including mobile (see Figure 14.1). Mobility is included here as one of the leading new delivery methods for digital and social media. Business leaders from PepsiCo to Facebook believe that smart mobile devices, such as the iPhone, Android, and other as-yet unimagined platforms, will remake the end user experience.[2] Kleiner Perkins partner Mary Meeker, famous for her detailed Internet and technology adoption statistics, notes that mobile is on track to be the primary method of user experience for the Web; in fact, in 2011, tablets and smart devices together outsold all PCs, including laptops. Mobile social networking is also accelerating this change as hundreds of millions of people shift their social media habits to entirely new devices and applications.[3]

Moving clockwise around the breakdown in Figure 14.1 gives a sense of the broad picture of the elements. Each element addresses one or more of the constituent audiences of social business.

Social Media Marketing

As one of the first major social business activities, social media marketing is a common activity in most organizations, with the majority

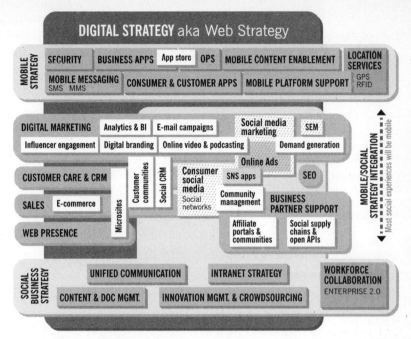

Figure 14.1   Putting Social Business into Context with Digital and Mobile Strategy

Note: SMS/MMS = short message service/multimedia messaging service; BI = business intelligence; GPS = global positioning system; RFID = radio-frequency identification; SNS = social networking service; SEM = search engine marketing; SEO = search engine optimization; API = application programming interface; E2.0 = Enterprise 2.0.

reporting successful results in a University of Massachusetts study conducted in 2010.[4] While social media marketing consists of a large number of practices, early adoption has been helped by the perception that it's the easiest and least risky to start with. The resulting early marketing focus has increasingly affected many related areas of digital strategy. Consequently, social media marketing is furthest along in the capabilities of many organizations, including areas such as community management, tool selection and use, and organizational design. One of the most significant challenges in this area remains the gap between push marketing and engagement marketing. Put simply, straightforward copying of push marketing techniques into social media channels doesn't work well. As explored in Chapter Six, the most effective results come from strategically engaging with the marketplace to jointly cocreate desired outcomes and network effects. Social marketing is now well beyond the early adoption phase, with 83 percent of Fortune 500 companies engaging in at least one social media service by late 2010.[5]

Demand Generation

A new aspect of digital marketing, demand generation consists of targeted digital awareness efforts to drive an understanding of and interest in a product or service. Primarily employed in business-to-business, public sector, and longer term business-to-consumer (B2C) sales cycles, demand generation involves multiple areas of marketing, including social media. It can be described as the fusion of marketing and sales into a holistic effort, using sophisticated support tools to combine data management and intelligence that allow community management of strategic marketing goals. Effective social business integration has also been appearing recently in off-the-shelf demand generation platforms such as those from Pardot, Marketo, and Eloqua, which can supplement and automate bespoke demand generation processes.

Search Engine Optimization

A long-term and vital component of Web strategy, search engine optimization (SEO) is as important as ever as the proliferation of content accelerates. With the volume and pace of content creation increasing—the vast majority being user generated—SEO is the intentional treatment of Web markup language to ensure that content is readily discoverable by search engines.[6] SEO is important externally as well as internally to an organization and remains a key aspect of digital strategy. It continues to evolve and expand as video, speech recognition (for audio), semantic, and social search engine optimization have become more commonplace. Social business strategies that don't have an SEO component will result in less discoverable information, lowering their return on investment.

Search Engine Marketing

Closely connected to SEO, search engine marketing (SEM) is the marketing aspect of the practice of optimizing information for discovery in order to promote Web sites and social media to increase their visibility for sales, branding, and other purposes.

Social Networking Applications

Interactive online experiences embedded into social networks have become increasingly common as engagement mechanisms, colocating branded user experiences within a broader social networking platform. By tapping into users' activity streams and social graphs, social networking applications have both the immediacy and full social context of their users to create a high-impact and shared social experience. Social networking applications exist for a wide range of purposes, including education, productivity, gaming, and marketing. Market leader Facebook has hundreds of thousands of available applications, and social apps are just now beginning to move seriously into the enterprise as well as through technologies such as Google-backed OpenSocial.

Online Advertising

Most businesses today have an online advertising strategy, usually underused in all but the most sophisticated Web industry firms where sophisticated multichannel tools and adaptive ad strategy are commonplace. For example, Amazon allows competitive ads on its own product pages, generating revenue on a momentary visitor impression, even if the customer decides to purchase the product someplace else. Advertising now goes beyond text ads to sophisticated user experiences that leverage rich media, social media, cross-platform

experiences, contests, and cocreation, and consists of carefully designed marketing funnels.

Consumer Social Media

The early world of consumer social media, consisting of blogs, wikis,
and simple social networks, has exploded into a sophisticated world of
global social networks, mobile applications, and aggregation involving most of the developed world. Social business strategy connects
to this complex landscape by exploring the many motivations and
options in engaging with consumer social media to create better
business outcomes.

Social Customer Relationship Management

As we explored in Chapter Nine, customer relationship management
(CRM) has been transformed by social media for a number of years.
Although the social media aspect of CRM is still early in its maturity,
CRM itself covers a wide range of activities, including sales, marketing, customer service, and technical support. Each of these aspects
benefits from the integration of social media. Presales Facebook
engagement, online support communities, and crowdsourced technical support are common uses of social CRM, with successful examples
including Get Satisfaction and FixYa showing that CRM costs can
be reduced while simultaneously increasing customer satisfaction
and loyalty.[7]

Customer Communities

Some leading examples of customer communities, such as HDTalking
for Harley-Davidson fans and the IKEAFANS community for Ikea
enthusiasts, are often created by customers, not the companies whose
products or services they support. Customer communities, which
started as little more than online discussion forums for tech geeks
in the early days of the Internet, have gone on to become a key
differentiator in the way that mainstream businesses engage with

their customers and the marketplace. In the social business era, the traditional corporate Web site, acting more as an online brochure instead of a way of participating in useful business activities with the marketplace, is being supplanted with more meaningful and productive aspects of customer engagement through the structured and unstructured activities of online and highly social communities.

Community Management

Making an impact on a number of areas of digital strategy, especially when social business is concerned, community management provides the necessary oversight, moderation, and support that social media need to drive initial adoption as well as remain successful and sustainable for the long term. Often informal and increasingly recognized as a key function, community management has been gaining respect as an indispensable capability of modern digital experiences that can lead to higher levels of success.

Affiliate Portals and Communities

As organizations look to scale their businesses using digital channels and labor costs limit their ability to meet business partner needs, they often discover that they don't have the staff to reach out and directly support thousands of trading partners, franchisees, and affiliates. Private label communities and social networks have become a prime tool in servicing these constituencies with a fraction of the staff. Frequently they lead to higher levels of awareness, engagement, service, and transaction levels than before.

Social Supply Chains and Open Application Programming Interfaces

Supply chain management has been one of the business functions least affected by social media, and it's one of the last areas of traditional business to be transformed with social business approaches. This is beginning to change, however, as we illustrated in the example

of Teva Pharmaceuticals in Chapter Three, which reported a manufacturing cycle time reduction of 40 percent as well as a reduction
in supplier lead time by up to 60 percent by applying social software
to communication challenges.[8] The closely related concept of open
supply chains, created by using simple application programming
interfaces and supported through developer communities, has led
to growing change in the way business partnerships are digitally
delivered and has been adopted by traditional organizations like Best
Buy, Sears, and the World Bank.[9]

Innovation Management and Crowdsourcing

The cocreation of ideas and peer production of work has become
highly scalable and dramatically less expensive as tool sets and
techniques have matured. A new crop of idea management services and platforms employing social business approaches, such as
Spigit, and crowdsourcing platforms like Crowdspring and Amazon's
Mechanical Turk have led to a small and steadily growing revolution
in the way businesses can collaborate directly with the marketplace
with their initial efforts or operational investment.

Workforce Collaboration

The use of internal social media, explored in detail in Chapter Eleven,
has become increasingly common. The manner in which social media
gain a foothold in organizations varies widely, often beginning in
social content management tools like wikis or getting started as an
internal corporate blog or other unsanctioned social tool. Corporate
communication departments are increasingly incorporating social
media into the company intranet as information can be found faster,
knowledge is retained better, and employees are more efficient and
productive when there is widespread social collaboration.[10]

Web Presence

Embraced by companies as one of the very first aspects of Internet
strategy, Web presence today includes rich media, mobile access,

e-commerce, software applications, self-service CRM, and now social media. Web presence is often located in a dedicated and frequently isolated project, next to, rather than integrated with, an organization's broader Internet strategy, since the platforms and tools on which it is based are either aging or technologically obsolete and are challenged in how they can enable the latest digital capabilities. Web presence remains a vital component of digital strategy, but its relevance is steadily being eroded by newer forms of engagement, including mobile applications and social business. Organizations can effectively reconcile newer digital strategy elements with legacy Web presence to create multichannel engagement strategies on their Web sites and elsewhere as they go up the engagement maturity ladder (see Figure 6.2).

Microsites

Microsites—Web sites publishing data focusing on a very specialized subset of company information—became increasingly common for targeted engagement as companies realized that customized digital communication was effective. Microsites remain an effective way to narrowcast online to a target audience or community to increase relevance, deepen reach, and foster engagement.[11]

E-Commerce

The growing dominance of e-commerce has steadily risen and is currently forecast to be a trillion-dollar business in the United States by 2014.[12] The latest developments include the rise of social commerce and daily deal services such as Groupon that connect discount e-commerce to local businesses, mobile e-commerce enabled by providers like Digby and Shopkick, and new payment systems, as well as social SEO (now the leader in driving inbound leads) and gaming.

Influencer Engagement

The idea that opinion makers and thought leaders can be engaged with indirectly to take advantage of the audiences they've created for themselves, rather than businesses recreating the engagement levels that individuals have already established with the market, is the concept behind influencer engagement. Often a key element of digital marketing strategy and an essential component of social marketing, influencer engagement is largely a manual activity because automated capabilities are still in early stages.

Analytics and Business Intelligence

Analytics and business intelligence across most aspects of digital strategy have emerged as a leading trend in the industry for their ability to derive useful insight and glean value from the social media relevant to the business. Companies can use emerging tools and techniques to work with vast quantities of data and make sense of the combined behavior of their workers, customers, and business partners. The resulting social business intelligence can make meaningful use of their collective knowledge to create competitive advantage.

Digital Branding

Despite fundamentally new forms of social engagement, the practice of developing and maintaining brand for establishing corporate and product identity remains a crucial aspect of digital strategy. This is true even as brands themselves are becoming increasingly influenced and defined directly by their customers. Peer-produced and cocreated marketing and advertising campaigns continue to proliferate as a result.

E-Mail Marketing

While e-mail is in slow decline in terms of use (see Figure 2.1), it remains an integral part of digital strategy for the foreseeable future. With its effectiveness dramatically reduced by the growth of e-mail spam and facing stiff competition from consumer, and now enterprise, social networks, e-mail is a less appealing channel now than it once was. However, as a notification tool, a viral feedback loop for social activity, and a useful touch point for multichannel CRM and marketing, e-mail is still necessary for social business.

Location-Based Services

As smart mobile devices become a leading way for the world to engage digitally, their global positioning sensors create opportunities to incorporate location awareness to drive marketing, sales, CRM, and operations. In the consumer world, geotagging of photos and the emergence of location-based social networks such as Foursquare have proven quite popular. While effective use of location remains in its infancy for most businesses, applied as part of a digital strategy, location awareness can drive improved personalization, useful geographical context, analytics, and process efficiencies for many types of business solutions.

Mobility Platform Support

Delivering service to internal users, trading partners, and customers means providing smart mobile-enabled solutions such as native mobile applications. Typically this means iOS and Android platforms for delivery of internal and external mobile applications. In order to deliver social business solutions on these new mobile devices, organizations must develop competency in mobile application development, operations, and management, as well as matching security, analytics, branding, advertising, and other related aspects of digital strategy.

Mobile Content Enablement

Enabling mobile use of existing information assets requires making existing content and user experience function optimally on the form factors and screens of mobile devices. Some of this process can be automated and is also usually less expensive and time-consuming than developing new mobile applications, though it can be less effective. Enterprises must consider the entire user experience including search, consumption, participation, and social business intelligence.

Consumer and Customer Mobile Applications

While the Web remains a crucial touch point, mobile applications are becoming a vital and important way to provide digital engagement, social and otherwise. For example, one of the most effective ways to engage with people under thirty years old is to have an application on the first or second screen of their smart mobile device.[13] Given the demographic trends, virtually all companies should be developing smart mobile capabilities for delivering digital engagement through mobile devices and ensure integration with the rest of their digital strategy.

Mobile Messaging

SMS (text) and MMS (images, audio, video) are among the most popular communication services in the world. However, they are threatened by the introduction of major new proprietary services such as Apple's iMessage service and a growing number of independent service providers, such as Pinger's popular Textfree app. Despite the technology's extensive history, organizations are only now beginning to absorb the lessons on how to employ mobile messaging for CRM and marketing and, to a lesser extent, soliciting user input such as surveys and other data collection. The growing market fragmentation of major new noncarrier messaging services provides opportunities to drive down the costs of using this channel just as it begins to lead channel proliferation challenges. Some early social media services, such as Twitter, began on mobile messaging services, and it can be a useful method of customer and worker engagement, especially for social business.

Mobile Line of Business Applications

Mobile application use inside organizations is rapidly growing, estimated at 15 percent per year in 2011.[14] Organizations are experiencing steady demand to provide existing services and solutions via electronic tablets and smartphones. While custom internal applications stores are a few years away for most organizations, building or buying mobile business applications is now well under way in many companies. Social media are readily available in mobile application form, and many applications now include social networking integration. Weaving social business capabilities into mobile applications focused on specific business processes or functions will become increasingly common.

Mobile Operations

Considerable operational capability and infrastructure development must be carried out, particularly with security and mobile management, in order to deploy smart mobile strategies in the enterprise. Bandwidth management for video chat is just one example of the challenges that mobile operations bring to the table. Social business strategies must anticipate capability levels and pursue funding to develop this area of the organization.

Mobile Applications Stores

Just as Apple set the expectation that mobile apps come from app stores, enterprises are now looking at enabling the same conduit. App stores are positioned to be a leading distribution model for both external and internal mobile applications. While these stores are already the primary way new applications are acquired on smart mobile devices, organizations have a considerable amount of work to do to resolve issues around data security, provisioning, and governance before they can open up stores inside their organizations to handle and use business data.

Mobile Security

Not part of digital strategy normally yet a required capability for internal use, mobile security is a key enabler and requirement for the move to mobile applications, particularly on platforms that are less controlled, such as Android. The priority with this capability is to ensure that customers and workers have a safe and effective mobile experience for those delivering through digital channels and social business solutions.

Content and Document Management

Social media have had a sustained and continuing impact on content and document management, to the extent that many of the latest iterations of these tools are major social platforms in their own right (Drupal is an example). Reconciling the proliferation of social media, content management, and document management platforms, many of which also connect to the public and have digital strategy implications, is one of the bigger challenges for enterprise information technology departments.

Intranet Strategy

Key to workforce engagement, intranet strategy is not typically part of traditional digital strategy, yet it is important as workers become more connected to customers and partners through digital channels, including social media. Social media are continuing to be adopted by more enterprise intranets; however, only a loose integration between digital strategy and intranet strategy exists in most organizations given the diversity of stakeholders. Social business strategies should include an intranet component for the workforce engagement part of their effort.

Unified Communications

Concerned with connecting all types of communication into a single coherent strategy, unified communications have considerable overlap with social media. Though lagging in social offerings, unified communications platforms and strategy now take social media into account.

Online Video and Audio

Rich media continue to grow as part of a robust and complete digital strategy, especially using social media, the leading source of rich media today. The emerging-growth areas that a social business strategy should focus on are in persistent multipoint video chat, video archival and search, mobile video, and transcription and SEO capabilities. Integration of video into digital experiences and mobile applications is also growing; for example, Facebook added Skype-powered video calling in July 2011, and Google+ allows users to connect in video "hangouts" using a mobile application. Rich media are believed to lead to better engagement and productivity.[15] Digital strategies that treat video as a driver of network effect and accumulated value growth will have the most significant long-term return on investment.

The challenge of taking such a broad-based perspective on the intersection of digital strategy and social business becomes finding and coordinating principals within an organization who can drive integrated strategy without slowing social business progress. As we explore in Chapter Eighteen, however, it's only by coordinating and supporting distributed action on the ground, enabling consistent yet widespread autonomous action via a social business unit, that an organization can implement social business in a controlled yet rapid manner.

Chapter 15

Business Cases, Pilots, Return on Investment, and Value

Tying Them Together

As social business enters a new stage of maturity after a half-decade of business application, a number of lessons learned stand out. Now that social media are no longer the shiny yet unknown objects of years past, more practical considerations have entered into social business discussions. The focus now is on how to create, manage, and govern social business communities successfully and sustainably. Businesses are also moving beyond initial experiments toward specific ways to deliver measurable business value. Perhaps most of all for middle to late adopters is a desire for proof and efficacy to learn what works best—and what perhaps does not—in social business.

Fortunately, the broad outlines of new social business models have emerged, along with the techniques to deliver on them successfully. Elements include business case, tool selection, worker policies, community management, and governance of social business environments. Just as important, as we have demonstrated throughout this book, companies large and small are now implementing social business at scale, providing valuable content for case studies as peers and partners embark on similar journeys.

We have seen the end of the beginning for social business. Lessons learned from developing business cases, operating pilots, and calculating return on investment have led to proof points for social business adoption (see Figure 15.1). Most large companies require detailed business cases for large investments, and these points can be instrumental in overcoming the questions and challenges for those preparing social business strategies for approval by corporate governance committees and boards of directors, who will have to stake their goodwill and reputation on the thoroughness and accuracy of the business cases that are put to them. Success metrics include:

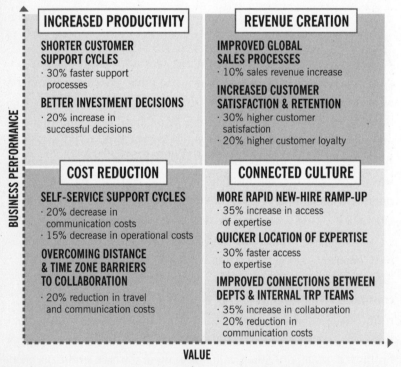

Figure 15.1 Ingredients of the Business Case: The Potential Return on Investment of Social Business

- *Higher productivity.* Research by Frost and Sullivan and the Mc-Kinsey data cited in Chapter One has made it clear that definitive productivity gains are achievable, including an average 15 percent decrease in operational costs to get the same work done and a 30 percent average increase in access to knowledge to get work done.[1]

- *Better access to experts.* Senior business leaders report a 35 percent increase in access to internal expertise.

- *Information discovery.* Information can be found more quickly (30 percent faster) in the open ecosystems of social business than in the trapped silos of traditional communication channels.

- *Business agility.* There is a surprisingly close relationship between social business and agile methods. The more transparent and participative processes of social business can provide substantially faster work cycles and feedback loops (30 percent average improvement).

- *Improved innovation.* Tapping into a broader pool of innovation using social media can lead to better products and improved services, but this is also one of the hardest types of improvements to quantify. A 20 percent increase in successful decision-making is one of the benefits, but it's the only unassailable quantifiable improvement to the innovation process—that is, deciding which innovations developed through social business methods processes to implement.

- *Competitive positioning.* An average 10 percent increase in sales revenue was reported. More successful innovation and higher productivity rates can create new products to move a company ahead of its competitors, while productivity can lower the cost of producing products. In some cases, dramatic cost reductions can be achieved by methods such as crowdsourcing, allowing breakthrough margin and pricing opportunities.

- *Workplace modernization.* The expectation by millennials, also known as Generation Y, the so-called next-generation workforce of those aged thirty and under, is very different from previous generations. They expect a work environment that is much more open and responsible than in the past and is always connected.[2] Social media are a leading activity of this demographic, the future of the workforce. Social business processes are a natural and expected part of the work landscape.

- *Higher levels of transparency.* A 35 percent increase in cross-functional collaboration, 20 percent increase in successful decisions, and 30 percent increase in access to knowledge are attributable to the openness and participative nature of social business solutions.

- *Less duplication.* Because of the higher levels of transparency inherent in social business approaches, one of the biggest anecdotal benefits reported by implementers is a reduction in duplicate work taking place in organizations.[3]

- *Better communication and collaboration.* A nominal 35 percent improvement in collaboration and a 20 percent reduction in communication and travel costs were reported by social business adopters.

- *Increased resilience to disruption.* Organizations using social business to drive mass participation in their business processes, from product development to customer care, should receive a direct benefit by having faster, more durable processes that are less susceptible to disruption by virtue of broader and more diverse inputs. Limited quantifiable data exist in this area, although early studies have shown promise.

- *Higher revenue and profit.* Numerous studies have shown that adopters of social business generate either higher revenue on average than companies that aren't fundamentally social, higher profits, or both. Although some studies show only a correlation, increasingly the evidence of a causal link is mounting.[4]

The pilot process is an ideal time to collect data about the benefits of a newly designed social business solution. While it's often much easier to use existing processes in place within a business to measure key performance indicators, the list above also provides useful guidance for crafting a business case on the likely returns, estimating the return on investment on an average basis (specific industry averages will vary, but supported data is not generally available), and identifying what to measure so that a case can be made to leave the pilot and provide a solution to a broader target audience.

Chapter 16

Building a Social Business Strategy

The Outputs

From the early years of experimentation and initial success stories, the first broad outlines of a genuine body of knowledge are emerging on how to make social business work effectively. So-called best practices and effective fundamental techniques have been identified and understood. Ideally, in addition to understanding the scope of comprehensive social business strategy, understanding how best to manage the upside while dealing with any potential downsides is necessary. New approaches and techniques for conducting business ultimately are codified into frameworks or methodologies, that is, systematic ways of identifying and applying methods for a given discipline. Operationalizing lessons helps new adopters identify and organize practices in a way that takes advantage of the experiences of pioneers and ensures that new efforts build safely on top of a tested body of community knowledge.

The first social business methods are now beginning to emerge, some explicitly but most implicitly, as practitioners assess their early successes and try to understand what worked well and what didn't occur as hoped.

We have introduced two major sets of social business concepts. The first are the ten tenets of social business, the ground rules for being successful regardless of the business activity, industry, audience, or demographic. The second is the process of social business transformation introduced in Chapter Thirteen. Combining the top-down and bottom-up drivers of social business transformation produces a set of core artifacts for communicating, guiding, and documenting the process. These are set out in Figure 16.1. Many organizations

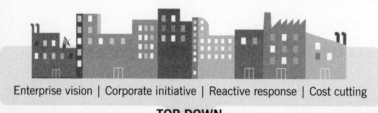

Enterprise vision | Corporate initiative | Reactive response | Cost cutting

TOP DOWN

SOCIAL COMPUTING PATTERNS & BEST PRACTICES	RISK MANAGEMENT & CHANGE MANAGEMENT
BUSINESS NEEDS & REQUIREMENTS	AD HOC OPPORTUNITIES
SOCIAL TOOLS, INFRASTRUCTURES, STANDARDS	SOCIAL BUSINESS NARRATIVE
SECURITY & IDENTITY STRATEGY	

COMMUNICATION PLAN

SOCIAL BUSINESS DESIGN

SOCIAL BUSINESS SUPPORT STRATEGY

SOCIAL BUSINESS STRATEGY & ARCHITECTURE

BOTTOM UP

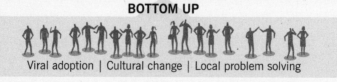

Viral adoption | Cultural change | Local problem solving

Figure 16.1   Social Business Initiative: Key Artifacts

use social business tools to create and maintain these artifacts, with community participants keeping them updated, relevant, and alive.

There are many secondary artifacts to any project: detailed requirements lists, software designs, coordination and project plans, testing reports, support cases, and others. But the key artifacts that are instrumental to the success of a social business effort are further explained in Figure 16.2. In particular, the ad hoc opportunities and social business narrative are explicit attempts at focusing on and extracting the most out of unique capabilities that set social business design apart from many prior innovations: emergent and peer-produced aspects leading to significant results. Not all social business efforts routinely apply all of these artifacts, even when they are successful. Social business strategies must tailor these artifacts for their needs and the requirements of local culture within an organization.

Artifact	Audience	Purpose
Business needs, goals, and objectives	Executives, stakeholders	Communicates business drivers of social business strategy
Social tools, infrastructures, and standards	Enterprise architects, developers, system integrators, third-party contractors	Identifies specific technical elements that will be used to create social business solutions
Security and identity strategy	IT security, business partners	Enumerates security issues and identifies approaches to address them
Social business design	Business owners, analysts, developers, testers, key end user stakeholders, community managers	Describes intended social business solutions to address outstanding business needs

Figure 16.2   The Critical Artifacts for Social Business Initiatives

Artifact	Audience	Purpose
Social business support strategy	IT help desk, customer support, community management	Outlines how community management and other supporting capabilities, such as listening and engagement, will operate and support social business strategy and resulting designs
Social business strategy and architecture	Business owners, executives, architects, project managers	Overarching description of the organization's social business strategy and its principles, aims, and long-term process
Ad hoc opportunities	Business owners, project management, key end user stakeholders	List of emergent social business outcomes and solutions that are candidates for further reinforcement, cultivation, scaling up, or other resolution
Communication plan	Executives, business owners, community managers, evangelists	Process that will be used to prepare audiences, inside and outside the organization, for transformation of processes with social business
Social business narrative	All	Ongoing conversation about high-level social business strategy as well as discussions specific to social business designs, fed back into social business design process

Figure 16.2 (*continued*)

Chapter 17

Getting Started with Social Business

Traditional organizations commonly perceive newly adopted social modes of participation, whether internal or external, as optional activities. This becomes a challenge particularly when the newly desired behaviors required by social business design are not clearly defined and supported by operations. Often the old way of working is left intact: workers collaborate and customers interact through legacy channels that are familiar and supported by long-standing process. Changing mind-sets to adopt a social business approach must be a conscious and deliberate activity, especially in the early days of implementing a social business design.

Clear and obvious motivations and incentives must align with the use of new tools to instill behavior change and sustain a new model of engagement as habits are rebuilt. Companies developing new social business efforts want a proven, reliable way to drive the adoption of social business strategy, whether workforce engagement, social media marketing, or social customer relationship management. However, as we have explored throughout this book, social media are not as controllable and deterministic as earlier methods. Social business participants must help sustain engagement, create value, drive direction, and build community as part of delivering a social business solution. Communities can't be owned or controlled in the way that workers or partners can, but they can be guided and inspired. This makes the process of improving adoption in social business a considerably different proposition from the way businesses used to engage before social media.

THE PHASES OF SOCIAL BUSINESS ADOPTION

Social business has definite and distinct stages of uptake and adoption, regardless of audience type, and they are adjusted to the state of maturity and overall rate of social business adoption in the organization. The techniques used depend on the size and age of the community collected around the social business process. Adoption strategies can be organized around four major stages of maturity (Figure 17.1):

1. *Early adoption.* The earliest and most sensitive stage, this is when only a core group of members is engaged and a weak network exists within a small sustaining community. Charter members

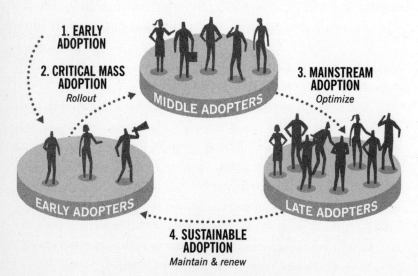

Figure 17.1 Phases of Social Business Adoption

must contribute to the hard work of cocreating the community, its processes, shared objectives, and expected behaviors. Adoption strategies during this stage focus on validation of direction, goals, and details of social business design. This is frequently known as the pilot phase.

2. *Critical mass adoption.* When the early adoption phase is successful, a deliberate decision usually is made to move into a self-sustaining situation. Until this time, considerable effort must be invested by the organization to recruit members able to draw in others and contribute themselves. When this is successful, critical mass becomes much easier to reach. Interestingly, research has shown that critical mass adoption can be as little as 10 percent of potential participants.[1]

3. *Mainstream adoption.* Typically a sustained gap occurs between the first two stages of adoption and late adoption. Early adopters are usually much earlier than the rest of the potential participants. Mainstream adopters usually have specific issues that are holding them back from adopting the social business solution—for example, skill gaps, poorly understood internal constraints, or even local laws or cultural expectations. In this stage, issues are systematically identified and steps are devised and carried out to resolve the remaining adoption issues.

4. *Sustainable adoption.* All communities decline over time without care and nurturing. To self-sustain, communities must be allowed to evolve without external restrictions. In the long term, workers leave the company, customers switch products, and companies change their services, and all of these affect long-term social business success. Community growth and health must be closely monitored, aided by the social business analytics processes typically in place at this time. Strategies to head off atrophy or drop in participation are devised and applied.

The remainder of this chapter focuses on a variety of adoption strategies; some apply across all stages of adoption, and others apply only during specific ones. Adoption strategies vary as much as companies do, however, and the social business transformation process will build this into the business process redesign as much as it does incentives and motivations for participants.

SOCIAL BUSINESS ADOPTION STRATEGIES

Adoption strategies for social business can be shared across a portfolio of social business efforts and then tailored to the local solution as needed. This is usually more efficient than reinventing the adoption strategies for each solution. Centralizing practices and knowledge drive the operational efficiency of the social business unit, which we discuss in the next chapter.

Internal Social Business Designs

Although the overlap between internal and external social business efforts is often considerable, most efforts are still separate. The top adoption strategies for internal social business efforts follow:

- *Establish a clear purpose.* Poorly articulated and vaguely designed social business efforts end up with matching outcomes. A clear purpose for an effort helps foster trust and sharing. When the high-level goals are explicitly identified, the audience can decide whether to join in and contribute to the social business process.
- *Identify and engage adoption champions.* One of the best ways to begin is to search out and identify natural leaders in the target community. Well-liked or respected members who participate early can spark the engine of viral adoption in the early adoption phase and encourage participation using social networks and good reputation.
- *Leadership sets the tone.* Leadership must clearly communicate how it wants workers to engage in and use social business solutions. Ideally leaders set personal examples through their own

participation. Public and sustained involvement by a handful of business leaders helps greatly.

- *Communicate clear policies for use.* Social business policies have evolved greatly. They have undergone refinement from complex, multipage statements to simple and clear directives. One of the biggest lessons learned is that employees must be informed of what they can or cannot do in clear terms. Done well, this removes uncertainty about when and how best to use different tools and communication channels and enables participation.

- *Validate social business design usability.* Just as with successful consumer products, social business designs must be easy to use. In fact, research has shown that a solution must be significantly easier to use than the solution it replaces in order for adoption to occur readily. Social business designs that aren't carefully tested with their users as simple and effective will have low productivity and high cost of use.[2]

- *Communication plan: A marketing campaign, consumer style.* Communicating features and benefits of social business solutions to workers helps set the baseline for how tools are perceived and subsequently used across the organization. Initial perceptions play a key role in adoption. Messaging must be useful and engaging while communicating improvements and incentives. One collaboration lead at a large multinational said: "Employees already have a preferred product. By using market segmentation and a value proposition for each 'segment,' we identified what they would need and how they wanted it delivered. A good customer doesn't just try your product; they buy it often and endorse it. Focus the sales on finding the 'good customers' and the best markets."[3]

- *Effective community management.* From the outset, community management (see Chapter Twelve) is one of the primary operational means used to foster the adoption of social business. Rachel Happe, a leading authority on community management, notes that "community building is a critical element of social business success and typically organizations cannot get there by deploying social technologies alone. There are a variety of contextual factors that can increase or decrease the ease of building a community but there are also some common best practices."[4]

- *Connect to the flow of work.* This is social business tenet 10. Instead of focusing social business approaches to a horizontal or general-purpose communications method that is competitive primarily with e-mail, educate users on how to improve a specific work activity or business process using a social method applicable to a given situation (for example, "When new sales results come in, post them to your activity stream, so everyone who wants to see can use them"). In general, the most effective results come from efforts that aim the adoption work (with matching social business designs) at a specific business process or challenge. As Laurie Buczek, a social media strategist at computer chip maker Intel, states, "First, identify the business objectives."[5]

- *Share the adoption process.* When the adoption process is open and members are encouraged and enabled to provide structure, share the rules of the road, and spread the word, they take ownership of the solution. Downstream, this results in more involvement and productive work. A key instance of this is SAP's Community Network, which uses a mentoring program to help enlist members to drive adoption through shared ownership.

External Social Business

When social business is used in external engagement with business partners and the general public, achieving adoption sometimes requires a complex blend of complementary adoption strategies. Some of these differences revolve around core motivations. For example, external participants are not usually remunerated by the organization in the same way that internal participants are. Consequently they have a very different set of reasons to get involved.

Additional concerns in external social business include having to engage a much broader demographic, as well as the competition with other communities targeting a similar audience. The top adoption strategies for external social business efforts are these:

- *Go to the audience, and draw them in.* A new Web site can be difficult for new participants to find and engage with. Existing networks support ready-made social and participative audiences; communities created in conjunction or connection with large social networks or other existing audiences can reduce early adoption challenges.
- *Employ unique content as a seed for participation.* Initially in most social business processes, something must be used to draw in and ignite engagement. Developing or purchasing seed content— information, data, or tools that participants will find immediately useful and usable—is a required investment. Member acquisition costs can be higher than expected if influencers are not well engaged early. Seed content is often used until an initiative reaches the critical mass phase of adoption.
- *Identify and enlist influencers.* As used in many digital strategy efforts, influencers have access to large, aligned audiences. Engage individuals with well-regarded reputations connected to the purpose of the social business effort. It's worth noting that engaging with influencers can take place in different ways, depending on the desired adoption effect (for example, retaining existing participants or acquiring new ones).
- *Solicit personal engagement from recognized business leaders.* Involving the targeted participation of company leaders can drive recognition for and engagement from the community. Providing participants with access to noted figures by recognized members of the community leads to the recognition and rewards that are more likely to increase adoption and lead to productive outcomes.

- *Reward the remarkable 1 percent.* As little as 1 percent of a community accounts for the majority of contributions to an effort.[6] The most valuable contributors must stay motivated and be rewarded appropriately. Rewards cover the range from simple recognition and acknowledgments to more formal business relationships.

- *Engage in community management.* As with internal business, community management is critical to the creation and maintenance of a vibrant and participative community. A leading community manager notes: "Organizations must allocate a full-time community manager that both encourages member activity and keeps the conversation on track."[7] Organizations often under-allocate the resources for this function, which is vital to social business adoption.

- *Keep it simple.* The social business design must be usable by the widest demographic audience. It must be easy to join, invite others, and participate in to cut down on user abandonment rates and maximize the value being exchanged.

- *Be authentic, and don't overpackage.* The most polished and professional social business experiences don't always achieve nearly the uptake as ones that are grounded and basic, and seem more personal. Too much polish conveys a sense of contrivance and control. The exception here seems to be social marketing experiences, which are often designed to visually impress.

- *Us first, the world second.* Organizations must have a distinct presence in the social business process and drive it forward. At first, it will be largely the company and its core advocates; as the company's participation creates a foundation of activity and value, others will join in.

- *Foster trust and a culture of sharing.* It's not sufficient to merely establish trust; a culture must be created where the free and open exchange of ideas is encouraged and rewarded. Creating such a culture requires leadership by example and reward for valuable contributions.

Adoption methods are very much in flux as social business becomes more formal and structured, yet powerful techniques are emerging. Social media can now be measured and monitored better than ever before. The rise of social business intelligence, explored in Chapter Twelve, provides the ability to measure and thus manage social business adoption. The cycle of listen, analyze, measure, and respond becomes a powerful tool to spot roadblocks and critical situations that are holding back or preventing adoption or causing retention and sustainment issues. Adoption must always be driven by people who are helping each other to succeed.

Chapter 18

Maturity

The Social Business Unit

As organizations take inventory of their growing portfolio of internal and external social media projects, they often open a Pandora's box of issues. Many are trying to get past the early learning years and their inevitable challenges, trying to determine how best to organize and deal with increasingly diverse and widespread activities. While individual employee efforts can and should be considered part of social business adoption, businesses realize that the era of isolated and tactical social media projects must change. It's not uncommon to see large global enterprises possessing hundreds of individual social media efforts, many coming as a surprise to centralized management.

The proliferation of social media use has become a high-priority issue as organizations seek to fund, standardize, and support social engagement across their lines of business. Organizations lack effective intellectual and operational control over their vast and frequently disconnected social media initiatives and effort. The outputs are clear: unnecessary duplication and inconsistent engagement with poor coordination, standardization, and economies of scale. Consequently organizations seek ways to consolidate, optimize, and focus combined social media efforts. That doesn't necessarily mean centralization, but more often a center of excellence to help govern efforts.

A new departmental entity, the social business unit, is forming in organizations undergoing widespread social media transformation. While the specific name used depends on organizational style, the unit might be an informal group inside corporate communications, or it could be a well-funded social media center of excellence created as a new entity on the organization chart. The social business unit facilitates social media adoption and use across the company by providing standards, best practices, lessons learned, coordination, and common capabilities such as community management and social business intelligence. Social business units help to reduce duplicative functions, rationalize social business infrastructure and applications, and combine and centralize certain social business functions where it makes sense. A social business unit also can coordinate results and lessons learned more coherently, efficiently, and in a timely way than receiving the status of several hundred individual projects.

The mission of a social business unit in any organization is clear: centralize what makes sense, support efficient adoption of social media through resource sharing and support, and enable emerging outcomes through best practices and lessons learned about how social business works best. Social business units typically assist in these ways (see Figure 18.1):

- *Competitive assessment.* Organizations need to keep close track of competitors in social business. Social media maturity varies widely by company, even in the same industry, and most companies can benefit from a regularly updated picture of their competitive context. Merely copying competitors is not the objective; rather, assessment uncovers opportunities for outperforming the competition. Customers' expectations are also set by how competitors engage, requiring competitive response. In some cases, social business engagement is a race to establish compelling customer communities in order to lock in loyalty and subsequent participation of a set of target customers first. A competitive assessment, updated regularly, can

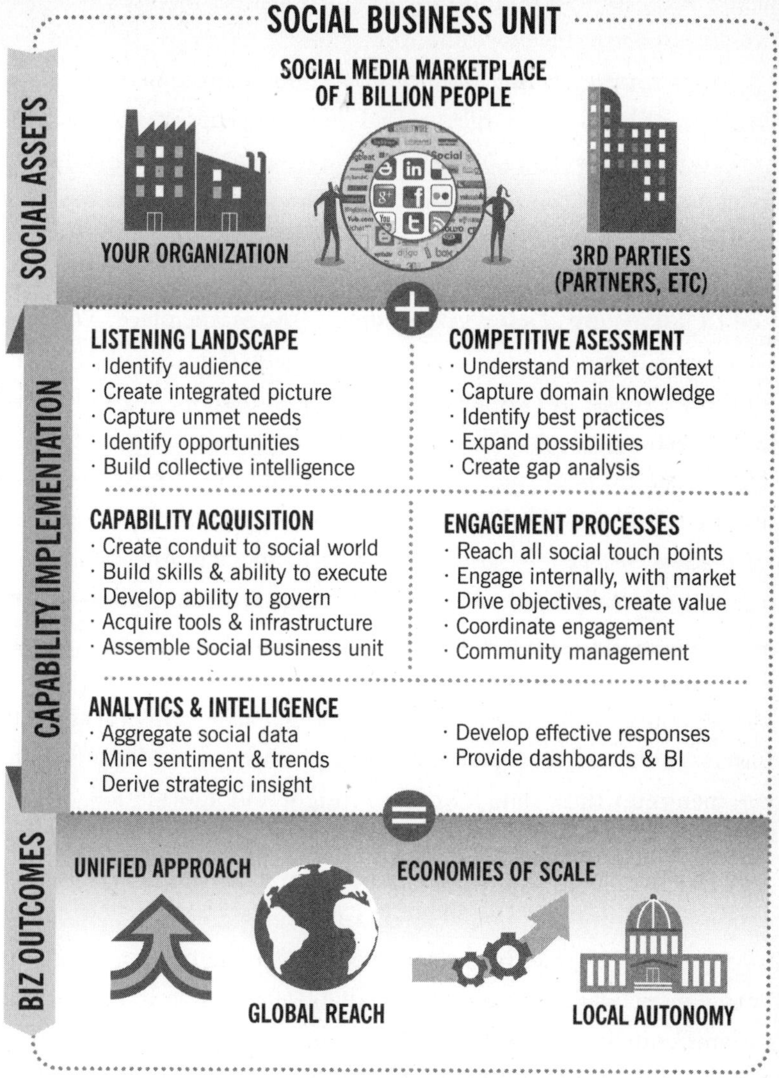

SOCIAL BUSINESS UNIT

SOCIAL ASSETS

SOCIAL MEDIA MARKETPLACE OF 1 BILLION PEOPLE

YOUR ORGANIZATION

3RD PARTIES (PARTNERS, ETC)

+

CAPABILITY IMPLEMENTATION

LISTENING LANDSCAPE
· Identify audience
· Create integrated picture
· Capture unmet needs
· Identify opportunities
· Build collective intelligence

COMPETITIVE ASESSMENT
· Understand market context
· Capture domain knowledge
· Identify best practices
· Expand possibilities
· Create gap analysis

CAPABILITY ACQUISITION
· Create conduit to social world
· Build skills & ability to execute
· Develop ability to govern
· Acquire tools & infrastructure
· Assemble Social Business unit

ENGAGEMENT PROCESSES
· Reach all social touch points
· Engage internally, with market
· Drive objectives, create value
· Coordinate engagement
· Community management

ANALYTICS & INTELLIGENCE
· Aggregate social data
· Mine sentiment & trends
· Derive strategic insight

· Develop effective responses
· Provide dashboards & BI

=

BIZ OUTCOMES

UNIFIED APPROACH

ECONOMIES OF SCALE

GLOBAL REACH

LOCAL AUTONOMY

Figure 18.1 Creating a Centralized Social Business Capability That Enables Local Action

help a business understand how it is performing and how to apply this knowledge to develop organizationally.

- *Social listening.* Many organizations spend most of their effort listening only to the largest social network ecosystems, such as Facebook and Twitter. The social business unit helps expand listening to the hundreds of relevant social networks and communities that host conversations relevant and important to a company. Many vertical and industry-specific online communities exist that must be tracked to build a full picture of what's happening in the marketplace. The flow of business opportunities, customer care situations, product ideas, and more reside in existing social media channels, lying fallow for firms that have the capability to listen over the social media landscape. The social business unit helps connect the resulting streams of information from listening to social business processes.
- *Analytics and business intelligence.* Once the social business unit has a listening capability, it must make sense of the vast and endless stream of business-critical knowledge flowing from consumer social media, as well as internal social business processes. The combined, integrated picture contains vital trends, business performance, and other data to form a connected and focused view of performance. Organizations can then mine these data for deeper insight and information.
- *Engagement processes.* Listening and analysis are important, but social media often require a response in the form of conversation or action by the organization. The social business unit can help create a consistent and effective companywide capability for social business engagement while coordinating with business units that have the responsibility for the business situation in question.
- *Capability acquisition.* Developing a social business unit requires time, investment, and political buy-in from a good portion of the organization. Although even the most mature examples are just a few years old, units usually undergo several phases as lessons are learned and the appropriate sets of resources, responsibilities, and processes are identified. Achieving a good balance between central

control of social media and autonomous (yet coordinated) local action can be an ongoing challenge, particularly as social media become more common across the business. Effective social business unit leaders are knowledgeable about their entire business, social business techniques, and how to operate effectively in the operational and political landscape of a large organization. They are also careful not to seek too much overt or unnecessary control over existing initiatives in the organization.

The social business unit is the best option for large enterprises to organize for social business. A growing number of organizations find them useful structures to deliver on social business in a controlled yet enabling way while tapping into valuable economies of scale and shared experience.

EPILOGUE

All organizations change and evolve. The speed at which they move depends on the industry and the nature of the business. Change is constant for businesses that wish to survive the procession of innovative technologies, workforce evolution, and changes in the marketplace. Throughout this book, we have provided the raw material for making a successful transition to social business, providing the background, foundational concepts, and organizing principles for typical organizations to begin making the transformation strategically. The good news is that it's no longer an act of faith. Social business successes of well-known, market-leading organizations offer compelling evidence of the returns on this next evolution of business. So too are the performance improvement numbers and return on investment established in studies and research efforts of social business approaches, as explored in Part One of this book. The implication of social business is that we are at the beginning of a new generation of enterprise that fundamentally operates better and creates significantly improved value to the world.

Yet even as the journey toward social business nears its first decade, many organizations have only begun their journey, and often in rather limited ways. This might seem surprising, given the benefits already known, the precedent by many industry leading firms, and ready access to techniques and tools. What, then, is holding companies back?

Several things, it turns out, and addressing these will be the central mission for social business transformation efforts. Social business entails deep changes in both strategic thinking and operational reality. This is often referred to as "changing one's DNA," and it can be difficult, yet, as difficult things often are, it is more than rewarding enough to make the attempt. *Social Business by Design* comes down to this one proposition: if companies can change the way they fundamentally work, a whole new set of benefits and opportunities is possible. Will you be the one to lead your organization toward social business? The way forward is literally in your hands.

Nevertheless, it turns out that there are a few classic yet unusually stubborn barriers that prevent innovations like social business from making rapid headway in the typical organization. Unless these barriers are largely overcome, it's unlikely that a company will move toward social business in a way that will make a competitive difference or sustainable contribution to the bottom line. In fact, the obstacles we identify are going to be some of the primary barriers to organizations as they make the transition to a social business. The call to action, to become a social business by design, means rallying the organization to change itself in unprecedented ways. Some companies are doing this now. Will yours be among them? Given the high impact that successful transformation to social business can have, it's likely that the future of your company depends on it.

The mind-sets behind major organizational obstacles to making the move to social business can be summarized:

- *Not invented here.* The tenets of social business are a foreign concept, especially in companies with closed, closely held cultures that are highly self-contained and don't value outside innovation.
- *The "boat" is too big to steer.* The larger the company, the argument goes, the more difficult it is to change direction and do something

new in a widespread way. Any major change would require too much expense or time.

- *A strong, distinct culture.* Companies with well-established, defined internal cultures can be high performers, yet the culture itself can often act as an immune system that throws out foreign invaders, such as new ideas that might threaten the culture.
- *Domination of short-term thinking.* Some companies are naturally crisis driven or highly reactive in nature, particularly to financial performance windows, putting them on a treadmill that prevents systematic, well-orchestrated change.

These fixed mind-sets are obstacles to all kinds of innovation and new ideas, not just social business. Although the solutions to overcoming these barriers will be as different as the nature of the individual companies trying to implement change, the solutions will all share key traits in common. First, they will be decentralized efforts with well-defined identities and objectives. They will also focus on constructive outcomes, discovered by engaging and listening to their ecosystems (customers, partners, and marketplace). Research has shown that the "immortals," companies that have lasted over at least one hundred years of constant change, consistently conduct business in a manner highly supportive of change and innovation.[1] We can learn from those that have changed over and over again, and we also know that social business can be successfully adopted, but only if the tenets are employed in a way that overcomes these natural, yet formidable, obstacles. Ultimately this requires making the first and most important step.

At the Dachis Group, we believe that social business is a natural, inevitable new way of working that taps into what makes us human and produces our best work with the broadest possible benefits to all participants. The network (the global Internet or your company network) now makes this readily possible for the first time in history, and it makes social business global frictionless and the easiest way to work—that is, if we can figure out how to escape the well-worn ruts of the old ways of working. This then is the signature challenge and call to action of the social business era. It's also your challenge as you proceed forward: as technology creates a widening gap between the early adopters and late arrivals, the only shortcut is to boldly push aside the outdated ways of doing business and openly cocreate new social businesses with solutions that drive change, both international and emergent.

Social business requires a minor revolution in thought and a steady evolution of cooperative action, but only if the initial and most critical step is confidently made with as little compromise as possible: *everyone is allowed to participate.*

APPENDIX: THE TEN TENETS OF
SOCIAL BUSINESS

Although no list of concepts about social business will ever be 100 percent complete, certainly some are more fundamental than others. To this end, the tenets listed below go directly to the heart of why social business is a highly effective and more potent new way of working. Together, these tenets represent a fundamentally open, participative, scalable, and rich way of living, working, and otherwise connecting and engaging with the world. As we presented in detail throughout this book, the use of these tenets, planned or otherwise, is making its way deep into the work processes, information technology systems, and business models of enterprises, transforming how they operate and achieve results.

The ideas of social business, as they appear in virtually all areas and functions of enterprises today, require clear and sustained focus and are improved by deliberate cultivation and intentional application to the key functions within the business. Although these tenets must be adapted to the specific needs of any organization, as they stand, they represent one of the most succinct and useful statements of what social business actually is, free of jargon or technology:

Tenet #1: Anyone can participate.

Tenet #2: Create shared value by default.

Tenet #3: While participation is self-organizing, the focus is on business outcomes.

Tenet #4: Enlist a large enough community to derive the desired result.

Tenet #5: Engage the right community for the business purpose.

Tenet #6: Participation can take any direction. Be prepared for it, and take advantage of it.

Tenet #7: Eliminate all potential barriers to participation. Ease of use is essential.

Tenet #8: Listen to and engage continuously with all relevant social business conversations.

Tenet #9: The tone and language of social business are most effective when they're casual and human.

Tenet #10: The most effective social business activities are deeply integrated into the flow of work.

NOTES

Chapter One

1. Finnern, M. "Office 2.0 Conference Panel: Online Communities." Sept. 24, 2007.

2. Happe, R. "Managing The Social Ecosystem: A SAP Case Study." Oct. 2010. http://community-roundtable.com/2010/10/managing -the-social-ecosystem-an-sap-case-study/.

3. Yolton, M. "BlogWell San Francisco Case Study: SAP." July 2011. http://www.slideshare.net/GasPedal/bw-sf2-sapss.

4. Johnston, S. J. "Microsoft Initiates Developer Network Service." *InfoWorld*, Aug. 1992, p. 8.

5. Klier, K. "From Community to Kinship: Online Communities That Drive Business Impact" (presentation at iStrategy Conference, Atlanta, Ga., Sept. 13, 2011). Klier is senior director of worldwide digital engagement at Microsoft.

6. Schroeder, S. "Old Spice: The Archetype of a Successful Social Media Campaign." July 2010. http://mashable.com/2010/07/15/old -spice-social-media-campaign.

7. Griner, D. "Hey Old Spice Haters, Sales Are Up 107%." *Adweek Online,* July 2010. http://www.adweek.com/adfreak/hey-old-spice-haters-sales-are-107–12422; "Old Spice Social Campaign Case Study Video." Digital Buzz Blog, Aug. 2010.

Chapter Two

1. Jacques, B., and Chui, M. "The Use of Web 2.0 in Businesses." *Financial Times,* Dec. 2010. http://www.ft.com/cms/s/0/c93e7bba-04a4–11e0-a99c-00144feabdc0.html#axzz1f7uQIrhz.

2. Wauters, R. "Over 1 Billion People Use Social Networks Today, and Other Stats." Sept. 2011. http://techcrunch.com/2011/09/14/over-1-billion-people-use-social-networks-today-and-other-stats/.

3. Ferraro, N. "Enterprises Should 'Design for Loss of Control.'" June 2010. http://www.internetevolution.com/author.asp?section_id=466&doc_id=193218.

Chapter Three

1. Jacques B., and Chui, M. "The Use of Web 2.0 in Businesses." *Financial Times,* Dec. 2010. http://www.ft.com/cms/s/0/c93e7bba-04a4–11e0-a99c-00144feabdc0.html#axzz1f7uQIrhz.

2. Verizon. "Meetings Around the World II: Charting the Course of Collaboration." Oct. 2009. http://www.verizonbusiness.com/resources/whitepapers/wp_meetings-around-the-world-ii_en_xg.pdf.

3. Network of Executive Women. "MillerCoors Taps Social Media to Retain More Women." Sept. 2011. http://www.newonline.org/news/72343/.

4. Miller, G. "Teva Supply Chain Gets a Boost from Social Media." FiercePharmaManufacturing. July 2011.

5. Miller. 2011.

6. Carr, D. F. "How Social Software Boosted Our Supply Chain ROI." June 2011. http://www.informationweek.com/thebrainyard/news/social_networking_private_platforms/231000274.

7. Traudt, E., and Vancil, R. *White Paper: Becoming a Social Business: The IBM Story.* Framingham, Mass.: IDC, Jan. 2011.

8. Traudt and Vancil. 2011.

9. WiseWindow. "Consumer Sentiment Measurement System Shows Near Direct Stock Price Correlation." Press release, Aug. 23, 2011. http://www.wisewindow.com/about-us/wisewindow-news/item /141-consumer-sentiment-measurement-system-shows-near -direct-stock-price-correlation.

10. WiseWindow. 2011.

11. Carr, D. F. "Social Media Stock Picks Come to Bloomberg." *InformationWeek,* Aug. 29, 2011. http://www.informationweek.com /thebrainyard/news/social_crm/231600420.

12. Freed, E. "Social Intranets: Not Just for Knowledge Workers." *Thought-Farmer Blog,* May 11, 2011. http://www.thoughtfarmer.com/blog /2011/05/11/social-intranets-not-just-for-knowledge-workers/.

13. Valentine, V. "Social Intranet Connects with Staff." *Information Management.* Aug. 12, 2011. http://www.information-management.com/news /social-intranet-connects-with-staff-10020940-1.html.

14. All, A. "Adding Social Elements to Intranet? Don't Forget Change Management." *IT Business Edge,* Aug. 16, 2011. http:// www.itbusinessedge.com/cm/blogs/all/adding-social-elements-to -intranet-dont-forget-change-management/?cs=48305.

15. Floyd, M. "Intuit's Live Community." *Slideshare.net,* May 2011. http:// www.slideshare.net/LucidImagination/morgan-floyd-intuits-live -community.

16. Ockham Research. "H&R Block Giving Way to Intuit." *Wall Street Pit,* Feb. 24, 2010. http://wallstreetpit.com/17613-hr-block-giving-way -to-intuit.

17. "Acquisitions Best Option for H&R Block: Activist Target Yet Again." *Seeking Alpha,* Oct. 19, 2011. http://seekingalpha.com/article/300469 -acquisitions-best-option-for-h-r-block-activist-target-yet-again.

Chapter Four

1. Kang, C. "Half of American Adults Use Facebook, Other Social Networks: Pew." *Washington Post,* Aug. 26, 2011. http://www .washingtonpost.com/blogs/post-tech/post/half-of-american-adults -use-facebook-other-social-networks-pew/2011/08/26/gIQA0PGGgJ _blog.html. Radicati, S., and Oh, D. *Social Networking Market, 2011–2015.* Radicati Group.

2. Bansal, S. "One Point for Crowdsourcing: Gamers Solve Protein Structure of AIDS-Like Protein." *Forbes*, Sept. 28, 2011. http://www.forbes.com/sites/sarikabansal/2011/09/28/crowdsourcing-gamers-solve-protein/.

3. Horowitz, B. "Creators, Synthesizer, and Consumers." *Elatable*, Feb. 16, 2006. http://blog.elatable.com/2006/02/creators-synthesizers-and-consumers.html.

Chapter Five

1. Jarvis, J. "Rupert Murdoch's Pathetic Paywall." *Guardian*, Mar. 26, 2010. http://www.guardian.co.uk/commentisfree/2010/mar/26/rupert-murdoch-pathetic-paywall.

2. Gunn, A. "Amazon Cuts Publishers Out of the Mix, Makes Deals with Writers." *PCWorld*, Oct. 18, 2011. http://www.pcworld.com/businesscenter/article/242095/amazon_cuts_publishers_out_of_the_mix_makes_deals_with_writers.html.

3. Hutchinson, A. "Human Resources: The Job You Didn't Even Know You Had." *Walrus*, Mar. 2009, pp. 15–16.

4. von Ahn, L. *NOVA ScienceNow*, season 4, episode 1, June 30, 2009. (Television program.)

5. Levine, R., Locke, C., Searls, D., and Weinberger, D. *The Cluetrain Manifesto*. New York: Perseus Books, 2000, p. 5.

Chapter Six

1. McNaughton, M. "77% of Fortune Global 100 Companies Use Twitter." *Real-Time Report*, Mar. 18, 2011. http://therealtimereport.com/2011/03/18/77-of-fortune-global-100-companies-use-twitter/.

2. Cockburn, A., Gutwin C., and Greenberg S. "A Predictive Model of Menu Performance." In *Proceedings of the SIGCHI Conference on Human Factors in Computing Systems*, San Jose, Calif., Apr. 28–May 3, 2007.

3. Shirky, C. "Wisdom on Crowds: What CEOs Need to Know About the Social Web." *Wall Street Journal Buzzwatch*, May 5, 2008. http://blogs.wsj.com/buzzwatch/2008/05/05/wisdom-on-crowds-what-ceos-need-to-know-about-the-social-web/.

4. Weingarten, M. " 'Project Runway' for the T-Shirt Crowd." *Business 2.0 Magazine,* June 18, 2007.

5. "BMW Recall Expands to 350,000 Cars." *CBS News,* Oct. 1, 2010. http://www.cbsnews.com/stories/2010/10/01/business/main6917 681.shtml; Bartlett, J. "Audi A3 Joins Volkswagen Golf, Jetta in TDI Recall for Fire Risk." *Consumer Reports,* Oct. 7, 2010. http:// news.consumerreports.org/cars/2011/10/audi-a3-joins-volkswagen -golf-jetta-in-tdi-recall-for-fire-risk.html; Massey, R. "Peugeot to Recall 7,000 Cars in UK over Accelerator Pedal Fears." *Mail Online,* Feb. 2, 2010. http://www.dailymail.co.uk/news/article-1247787/Peugeot -recall-7–000-cars-UK-accelerator-pedal-fears.html; Leach, B. "Peugeot Citroen to Recall Cars over Safety Fears." *Telegraph,* Jan. 31, 2010. http://www.telegraph.co.uk/motoring/news/7114267/Peugeot -Citroen-to-recall-cars-over-safety-fears.html; "Honda Recall 2010." *MyFox New York,* Jan. 29, 2010. http://www.myfoxny.com/dpp/news /consumer/dpgonc-honda-announces-worldwide-recall-of-646000 -cars-fc-201001291264789766773.

6. Chowney, V. "A Look at Toyota's Social Media Reputation with Web-trends." *ReputationOnline,* Feb. 12, 2010. http://reputationonline.co .uk/2010/02/12/a-look-at-toyotas-social-media-reputation-with -webtrends/.

7. Lawson, S. "Toyota Also Needs to Recall Social Media Strategy." *Friendly Voice,* Feb. 17, 2010. http://www.friendlyvoice.com /toyota-also-needs-to-recall-social-media-strategy/.

8. YouGov BrandIndex. "Toyota Freefall Following Vehicle Recalls." *BrandIndex,* Sept. 2, 2010. http://www.brandindex.com/article/toyota -set-suffer-long-term-brand-damage-following-vehicle-recalls.

9. Gilbert, S. "Meet 'Leroy Stick,' BP's Biggest Social Networking Rival." *Daily Finance,* June 8, 2010. http://www.dailyfinance.com/2010/06 /08/meet-leroy-stick-bps-biggest-social-networking-rival/.

10. Stick, L. (pseudonym). "Destroying the Gulf for: 87 Days." 2010. http://twitter.com/BPGlobalPR.

11. Kapin, A. "Can Ford's New Social Media Strategy Help It Become the Leading Social Automotive Brand?" *Fast Company,* Jan. 19, 2009.

http://www.fastcompany.com/blog/allyson-kapin/radical-tech/can
-fords-new-social-media-strategy-help-company-be-leading-social-a.

12. Oaks, J. "Our (My) Agreement with Ford (Remedy)." *TheRangerStation,*
Dec. 10, 2008. http://web.archive.org/web/20090220174525
/http://www.therangerstation.com/forums/showthread.php?p
=274763.

13. George, B. "Dell Opens Its Social Media Command Center." *Inside
Enterprise IT,* Dec. 16, 2010. http://en.community.dell.com/dell
-blogs/enterprise/b/inside-enterprise-it/archive/2010/12/16/dell
-opens-its-social-media-command-center.aspx; Read, B. "Time
Warner Deploys Social Media to Communicate with Customers." *Outbound Call Center,* Mar. 25, 2010. http://outbound-call-center.tmcnet
.com/topics/outbound-call-center/articles/79865-time-warner
-deploys-social-media-communicate-with-customers.htm.

Chapter Seven

1. Linton, Matysiak & Wilkes. *Marketing: Witchcraft or Science Report.* 2010.

2. Rich, L. "Tapping the Wisdom of the Crowd." *New York Times,* Aug. 4,
2010. http://www.nytimes.com/2010/08/05/business/smallbusiness
/05sbiz.html.

3. Battelle, J. "The Database of Intentions." *John Battelle's SearchBlog,*
Nov. 13, 2003. http://battellemedia.com/archives/2003/11/the
_database_of_intentions.php.

4. LG Electronics MobileComm U.S.A. "LG Mobile Phones Announces
Winners of 3rd Annual Design the Future Competition." *PRNewswire,*
June 1, 2011. http://www.prnewswire.com/news-releases/lg-mobile
-phones-announces-winners-of-3rd-annual-design-the-future
-competition-95305979.html.

Chapter Eight

1. Alexa. "Alexa Top 500 Global Sites." Nov. 2011. http://www.alexa
.com/topsites.

2. "Top 20 on 20 History." *Wikipedia,* 2011. http://en.wikipedia.org/wiki
/Top_20_on_20.

3. Open Innovators. *List of Open Innovation and Crowdsourcing Examples*. Jan. 2008. http://www.openinnovators.net/list-open-innovation -crowdsourcing-examples/.

4. Mitskaviets, I. *North American Technographics Consumer Technology Online Benchmark Recontact Survey, Q2 2010 (US)*. Cambridge, Mass.: Forrester Research, June 2010.

Chapter Nine

1. Bower, K. "Marketing Research Chart: Social CRM Is Increasingly Important for Managing Social Customer Relationships." *Marketing-Sherpa*, Oct. 18, 2011. http://www.marketingsherpa.com/article.php? ident=32036.

2. Gartner. "Gartner Says the Market for Social CRM Is on Pace to Surpass $1 Billion in Revenue by Year-End 2012." *Gartner Newsroom*, Aug. 30, 2011. http://www.gartner.com/it/page.jsp?id=1777938.

3. "About Page of Get Satisfaction." *GetSatisfaction*, Nov. 2011. http:// getsatisfaction.com/team/about.

Chapter Ten

1. Fredricksen, C. "Case Study: American Express OPEN Forum Socializes Small Business." *eMarketer*, May 13, 2010. http://www .emarketer.com/blog/index.php/case-study-american-express-open -forum-social-media-small-business/.

2. Roen, S. "Case Study: OPEN Forum." Presentation at the Signal LA Conference, Los Angeles, Feb. 9, 2011. http://www.slideshare.net /fmsignal/case-study-open-forum-scott-roan.

3. Indvik, L. "L'Oreal Teams Up with Buddy Media to Help Local Salons Market on Facebook." *Mashable Business*, Mar. 10, 2011. http://mashable.com/2011/03/10/loreal-facebook-buddy-media/.

4. Singer, M. "L'Oreal Sets Salon Appointments on Facebook." *All Facebook*, Apr. 20, 2011. http://www.allfacebook.com/l%E2%80% 99oreal-sets-salon-appointments-on-facebook-2011−04.

5. Forrester Research. "Forrester Research Announces 2011 Forrester Groundswell Award Winners For Excellence In Social Technologies." *Business Wire*, Oct. 28, 2011.

6. Rollstream. Customer Case Study: Owens and Minor. 2009. http://rollstream.com/assets/cs/cs_owensminor_2009.pdf.

7. Kelly, K. "The Shirky Principle." Technium, Apr. 2, 2010. http://www.kk.org/thetechnium/archives/2010/04/the_shirky_prin.php.

8. Prize4Life. "Prize4Life Awards $1M ALS Biomarker Prize!" Feb. 7, 2011. http://www.prize4life.org/page/news/6467.

9. Tapscott, D. *Wikinomics*. New York: Penguin, 2006.

10. Allarakhia, M. "GSK's Centres for Excellence in External Drug Discovery." Apr. 2011. www.bioendeavor.net/newsUrl.asp?nId=294660.

11. Roth, G. "GSK's New Unit May Change the R&D Outsourcing Game." *Contract Pharma*, Jan. 22, 2010. http://www.contractpharma.com/issues/2010–01/view_features/newsmakers-scinovo/.

12. Baker, H. "Case Study: Hewlett Packard." *B2B Guide to Social Media*. Mar. 24, 2011. http://www.b2bsocialmediaguide.com/2011/05/24/case-study-edelman/.

13. Cohen, J. "Pitney Bowes Uses Forums for B2B Customer Service." *Social Media B2B*, Sept. 25, 2009. http://socialmediab2b.com/2009/09/pitney-bowes-uses-forums-for-b2b-customer-service/.

Chapter Eleven

1. McAfee, A. "Enterprise 2.0: The Dawn of Emergent Collaboration." *MIT Sloan Management Review*, Apr. 1, 2006. http://sloanreview.mit.edu/the-magazine/2006-spring/47306/enterprise-the-dawn-of-emergent-collaboration/.

2. Twiki. "TWiki Success Story of Morgan Stanley." Sept. 28, 2011. http://twiki.org/cgi-bin/view/Main/TWikiSuccessStoryOfMorgan Stanley.

3. Keitt, T. J. "Is Social Software Relevant to Information Workers?" *ZDNet*, Forrester Research, Aug. 23, 2011. http://www

.zdnet.com/blog/forrester/is-social-software-relevant-to-information
-workers/713.

4. Simeonov, S. "Metcalfe's Law: More Misunderstood Than Wrong?" *HighContrast,* July 26, 2006. http://blog.simeonov.com/2006/07/26 /metcalfes-law-more-misunderstood-than-wrong/.

5. Reed, D. "The Law of the Pack." *Harvard Business Review,* Feb. 2001, pp. 23–24.

6. Poe, M. "The Hive." *Atlantic Monthly,* Sept. 2006. http://www.theat lantic.com/magazine/archive/2006/09/the-hive/5118/.

7. Rector, L. H. "Comparison of Wikipedia and Other Encyclopedias for Accuracy, Breadth, and Depth in Historical Articles." Library and Instructional Resources, Harford Community College, 2008.

8. Jacques, B., and Chui, M. "The Use of Web 2.0 in Businesses." *Financial Times,* Dec. 2010. http://www.ft.com/cms/s/0/c93e7bba -04a4–11e0-a99c-00144feabdc0.html#axzz1f7uQIrhz.

9. Kaplan, R., and Norton, D. *Strategy Maps.* Boston: Harvard Business School Press, 2004.

10. Bryant, L., and others. *Enterprise 2.0 Study D4: Final Report.* Dec. 7, 2010, p. 32.

Chapter Twelve

1. Twiki. "ReputationPlugin." Oct. 18, 2011. http://twiki.org/cgi-bin /view/Plugins/ReputationPlugin.

2. Lawley, S. "Finding the Right Person Within Your Organization." *Enterprise Web 2.0,* Aug. 19, 2011. http://www.zdnet.com/blog /hinchcliffe/finding-the-right-person-within-your-organization/1669.

Chapter Thirteen

1. McAfee, A. "Enterprise 2.0: The Dawn of Emergent Collabora-tion." *MIT Sloan Management Review,* Apr. 1, 2006. http://sloanreview .mit.edu/the-magazine/2006-spring/47306/enterprise-the-dawn-of -emergent-collaboration/.

2. McAfee, A. "Drop The Pilot." *Andrew McAfee's Blog*, Apr. 22, 2010. http://andrewmcafee.org/2010/04/drop-the-pilot/.

Chapter Fourteen

1. Mack, G. "Facebook Overtakes MySpace." *Alexa Blog*, May 7, 2008. http://blog.alexa.com/2008/05/facebook-overtakes-myspace_07 .html.

2. Butcher, D. "PepsiCo Exec: Majority of Social Interaction Will Happen via Mobile." *Mobile Marketer,* Feb. 14, 2011. http://www .mobilemarketer.com/cms/news/social-networks/9071.html.

3. Schonfeld, E. "Ramping Up: Mary Meeker's Latest Mobile Trend Slides." *Techcrunch.* Feb. 20, 2011. http://techcrunch.com/2011/02 /10/meeker-mobile-slides/.

4. Schaefer, M. "Research Shows Fastest-Growing Businesses Pile On to the Social Web." Grow, Feb. 17, 2010. http://www.businesses grow.com/2010/02/17/research-shows-fastest-growing-businesses -pile-on-to-the-social-web/.

5. Hameed, B. "Social Media Usage Exploding Amongst Fortune 500 Companies." *Social Times,* Jan. 21, 2011. http://socialtimes.com/social -media-usage-exploding-amongst-fortune-500-companies_b35372.

6. Hinchcliffe, D. "On Web Strategy." June 29, 2011. http://dionhinch cliffe.com/2011/06/29/on-web-strategy/.

7. Hinchcliffe, D. "When Online Communities Go to Work." Mar. 22, 2010. http://www.zdnet.com/blog/hinchcliffe/when-online-commu -nities-go-to-work/1342.

8. Carr, D. F. "How Social Software Boosted Our Supply Chain ROI." *InformationWeek,* June 23, 2011. http://www.informationweek.com /thebrainyard/news/social_networking_private_platforms /231000274/how-social-software-boosted-our-supply-chain-roi.

9. Best Buy. "BBY Open: Start Making." https://bbyopen.com/devel -oper; Sears. "APIs." Sears Developer Network. http://developer.sears .com/apis; World Bank. "About the API." For Developers. http:// data.worldbank.org/developers.

10. Nielsen, J. "10 Best Intranets of 2011." *Jacob Nielsen's Alertbox,* Jan. 4, 2011. http://www.useit.com/alertbox/intranet_design.html.

11. Crum, C. "Microsites Drive Brand Engagement, Purchase Intent." *WebProNews,* Apr. 2010. http://www.webpronews.com/microsites -drive-brand-engagement-purchase-intent-2010–04.

12. Frank, J. B. "E-Commerce + M-Commerce = $1 Trillion by 2014." *ePayment News,* Oct. 10, 2011. http://epaymentnews.blogspot.com /2011/10/e-commerce-m-commerce-1-trillion-by.html.

13. Dachis Group. Research citation at presentation at Social Business Summit, Singapore, Apr. 2011.

14. Research and Markets. "Global Mobile Enterprise Applications Platform Market, 2010–2014." *Fierce Wireless,* Apr. 1, 2011. http:// www.fiercewireless.com/press-releases/research-and-markets-global -mobile-enterprise-applications-platform-market.

15. Guerin, T. "Telstra Polycom Video Conferencing Case Study." *Slideshare,* Nov. 2010. http://www.slideshare.net/Turloughg/telstra -polycom-video-conferencing-case-study.

Chapter Fifteen

1. Turek, M. "Justifying the Cost of Social Media in the Enterprise." *NoJitter,* Feb. 21, 2011. http://www.nojitter.com/blog/229219010.

2. McLoughlin, A. "IT and the Millennials: Bridging the Chasm." *AIIM Social Business Expert Blog,* Apr. 19, 2011. http://www.aiim.org /community/blogs/expert/IT-and-the-Millennials-Bridging-the -chasm.

3. Freed, E. "Real Intranet Managers: Emily Staresina's Lessons Learned from Going Social." *Thoughtfarmer Blog,* Oct. 10, 2011. http:// www.thoughtfarmer.com/blog/2011/10/10/real-intranet-managers -emily-staresinas-lessons-learned-from-going-social/.

4. Dignan, L. "Does Social Media Really Correlate with the Bottom Line? Color Me Skeptical." *Between the Lines, ZDNet,* July 21, 2009. http://www.zdnet.com/blog/btl/does-social-media-really-correlate -with-the-bottom-line-color-me-skeptical/21413.

Chapter Seventeen

1. "Minority Rules: Scientists Discover Tipping Point for the Spread of Ideas." *Physorg.com,* July 25, 2011. http://www.physorg.com/news /2011–07-minority-scientists-ideas.html.

2. Nielsen, J. "Intranet Usability Shows Huge Advances." *Jakob Nielsen's Alertbox,* Oct. 9, 2007. http://www.useit.com/alertbox/intranet -usability.html.

3. Personal communication with John Woodworth of 3M Lab Collaboration, Aug. 2011.

4. E-mail conversation with Rachel Happe, founder of the Community Roundtable, Aug. 2011.

5. Fidelman, M. "9 Sure Fire Ways to Become a Social Business." *Seek Omega,* Aug. 10, 2011. http://www.seekomega.com/2011/08/the -social-phd-9-sure-fire-ways-to-become-a-social-business-video/.

6. Nielsen, J. "Participation Inequality: Encouraging More Users to Contribute." *Jakob Nielsen's AlertBox,* Oct. 9, 2009. http://www.useit.com /alertbox/participation_inequality.html.

7. E-mail conversation with Rachel Happe.

Epilogue

1. Gray. D. "The Connected Company." Austin, Tex.: Dachis Group Collaboratory, Feb. 9, 2011. http://www.dachisgroup.com/2011/02 /the-connected-company/.

ACKNOWLEDGMENTS

Writing a book about a topic that's changing so quickly is a difficult task, but it's been made much easier by the connection we've had to our coworkers and industry colleagues, both in-person and online, in social media. It's inevitable that we'll leave people out here who shouldn't have been, and for those we do, we hope to make it up in subsequent notes in social media and elsewhere.

First and foremost, we thank Jeff Dachis, CEO of Dachis Group, our employer, for allowing us to take the time to write this book and create such a complete yet distilled view of social business. Our editor, Karen Murphy, tirelessly pushed us to get this done, and done as well as it possibly could be. We'd be sorely remiss without listing those who drove the early conversations that continue to inspire and influence us, as well as creating the foundational thinking of the industry in its early years, including Andrew McAfee, John Hagel, Charlene Li, JP Rangaswami, Sameer Patel, Tim O'Reilly, Josh Bernoff, Ross Dawson, Sandy Carter, Ross Mayfield, Rachel Happe, Susan Scrupski, Jeremiah Owyang, Luis Suarez, David Armano, Jevon MacDonald, Lee Bryant, Dave Gray, and Clay Shirky.

We also thank the real-life practitioners who have moved the practice of social business forward and have informed the principles in this book through their work in the field. They include Mark Yolton, Sherri Maxson, Marisa Thalberg, Dan Beranek, Laurie Buczek, Bert Sandie, Kirk Kness, Mitchell Rose, Steve Lawley, Michael Donnelly, and Yuvi Kochar.

Those who helped us produce this book have been amazing as well, especially Bill Keaggy, who developed the figures throughout this book with the Dachis Group XPLANATiONS process. Support to make this happen came from our colleagues, including Kate Niederhoffer, David Mastronardi, Amanda Johnson, Chad Costello, and April Downing, who provided data or much-needed legal, contract, and logistical support.

Final thanks go to those who provided personal support and give us a reason for doing what we do. For Dion, that's Kate Allen. For Pete, they are Barbara, Mackensie, and Caroline.

ABOUT THE AUTHORS

Dion Hinchcliffe is executive vice president, strategy, of Dachis Group. As an enterprise architect, author, blogger, and business strategist, he works with the leadership teams of Fortune 500 and Global 2000 firms to devise strategies to help them adapt their organizations to the challenges and opportunities of the twenty-first century. He has been featured or quoted in *CIO Magazine*, *Computerworld*, *Forbes*, *Wired*, and *BusinessWeek* and is a frequent keynote speaker at industry-leading conferences such as Web 2.0 Expo, Enterprise 2.0, CeBIT, and the Agile Executive Forum. Hinchcliffe has previously cofounded and operated several thought-leading information technology and management consulting firms, including Hinchcliffe & Company and Sphere of Influence, where he broke new ground in the areas of next-generation information technology, social media, open supply chains, business agility, and emergent Web architectures for large enterprises. He writes about next-generation business at dionhinchcliffe.com and on Twitter at @dhinchcliffe.

Peter Kim is chief strategy officer of Dachis Group. As an advisor on social business, he works with clients on strategy formulation and driving global industry discourse. He has been quoted by media outlets including CNN, CNBC, NPR, the *New York Times,* and the *Wall Street Journal* and has been a featured speaker at events including SXSW, Web 2.0 Expo, and Dachis Group Social Business Summits. Kim was previously an analyst at Forrester Research and head of international marketing operations, e-commerce, and digital marketing at PUMA AG. He holds degrees from the University of Virginia Darden School of Business and the University of Pennsylvania. He blogs about social business at http://beingpeterkim.com and on Twitter as @peterkim.

Dachis Group powers social business performance for the world's leading companies, measuring social performance with social business intelligence, managing social brands with performance brand marketing, and redesigning social enterprises as connected companies. With its combination of a proprietary big data analytics platform, a comprehensive set of software-as-a-service social engagement technology platforms, and a world-leading social business professional services group, large companies rely on the company's counsel to establish powerful, effective, meaningful, and measurable engagement initiatives throughout their organizations. For more information, visit www.dachisgroup.com.

To join the ecosystem of social business practitioners and access additional information about social business, visit www .socialbusinessbydesign.com.

INDEX